The Little Best Dress

*Make the perfect little
dress for a BIG occasion*

Simon Henry

GUILD OF MASTER
CRAFTSMAN PUBLICATIONS

First published 2010 by

THE GUILD OF MASTER CRAFTSMAN PUBLICATIONS LTD

166 High Street, Lewes, East Sussex, BN7 1XU

For our own princess,
Nikisha, our very special
little girl.

ISBN 978-1-86108-687-7

A catalogue record of this book is available from the British Library.

Associate Publisher **JONATHAN BAILEY**
Production Manager **JIM BULLEY**
Managing Editor **GERRIE PURCELL**
Senior Project Editor **DOMINIQUE PAGE**
Copy Editor **RACHEL NETHERWOOD**
Managing Art Editor **GILDA PACITTI**
Photographer **CHRIS GLOAG**

Colour origination **GMC REPROGRAPHICS**
Printed and bound by **HING YIP PRINTING CO. LTD, IN CHINA**

Foreword

DO YOU REMEMBER WHEN YOU WERE A LITTLE GIRL and you always had a 'best dress'? One that was reserved for special occasions – weddings, parties, family functions – and you just couldn't wait for the next one so that you could be a princess all over again?

Imagine if you could have been a part of the design process for your own best dress: helping to choose the colour and the fabric; deciding on hem lengths; train or no train; sleeves or no sleeves. Now imagine giving your own little princess that opportunity without having to visit an expensive couturier or dressmaker. Imagine designing and making a new best dress for each and every occasion she attends.

Well, now you can. In this book I will show you, in easy-to-understand steps, how to make a pattern that fits, and then how to convert and manipulate that pattern into different styles of occasion dress, limited only by your imagination.

I will show you different bodice, skirt and sleeve styles that all work together, so that you and your princess can put them together in any combination that you like. Even if you have never sewn a stitch before I can assure you that, if you follow the instructions in this book methodically and systematically, you will be able to become your child's very own special-occasion dress designer!

Simon Henry

Contents

Rose p.100

Bluebells p.116

Lavender p.144

Lily p.154

How to Use This Book

It's really very easy to use this book: start at the beginning and work your way through. But even if you have done some sewing before, don't assume that I will be using the same methods that you have in the past. Read the basic sewing section for some valuable catch-up practice and to get used to my method of doing things.

My method of designing, cutting and sewing has been tried and tested on many students. I have cut out all the unnecessary steps that most home sewers hate. There is no tacking or basting. All of the fittings are done using calico so there should be minimal unpicking on the real garment. I even teach you to sew over the pins!

I can see all of the machine manufacturers and my fellow designers throwing their hands up in horror at this, but I can only

Little Tip

When anyone asks where you got your fabulous dress simply reply, 'Actually, it's home couture and I helped design it!' and remember, always be as precocious as possible!

answer any critics out there by saying: it works! I'm not teaching you to do this for a living (even though some of my students have gone on to be professional dressmakers), I am teaching you to make your little princess a gown, of which both you and she can be proud.

It would be lovely if doing these projects with your princess stimulates her interest in sewing and design. Who knows, perhaps one day she will be making a dress for you!

Happy sewing!

1 Getting Started

'Little girls are precious gifts, wrapped in love serene. Their dresses tied with sashes and futures tied with dreams.'

AUTHOR UNKNOWN

Equipment and Materials

Gather all of your equipment together before you start so you can get on with the job without stopping to look for missing items. Clear a space for yourself, lock out the children and the cat, and let's make a start.

Sewing machine

Auction websites are also good for second-hand machines. But, if you go down this road, be sure to have it professionally serviced so that it runs smoothly and the tension is set correctly. Buy new needles to suit individual fabrics.

Whatever you do, don't be tempted to buy an industrial machine just yet. They run too fast and you don't have the same control as a domestic one. If your machine has an adjustable speed, start with it on slow or medium until you are confident that you can control a straight stitching line – then you can gradually begin to increase speed.

Sewing machine

As long as your machine sews both straight stitch and zigzag, you will be able to follow the methods in this book.

Over the years, I have upgraded to the most advanced machines, spending thousands of pounds on the latest computer embroidery technology. To be honest, though, most of the time I only use the straight and zigzag stitches. If you don't have a machine yet, get hold of a basic one. Your local supplier will recommend something suitable – either new or used.

Take long strips of some waste fabric and practise sewing seams with a ⅜ in (1.5cm) seam allowance. Press the seam open and check that there is no pulling or puckering. If there is, adjust the tension setting on your machine to compensate. Refer to the operating manual for individual machines, as they will all vary slightly.

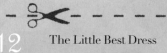

Overlocker or serger

An overlocker is very useful for finishing off seams and neatening hems, but is by no means an essential piece of equipment. You can finish seams very well by using the zigzag setting on your normal machine. If you are lucky enough to have access to an overlocker, practise stitching long strips of waste fabric before pressing with a steam iron. Check that the seam is not gathered or stretched. If so, adjust the tension according to the manufacturer's instructions.

The dress stand

A dress stand or tailor's dummy isn't really necessary for the projects in this book, but it can be very helpful, especially if your princess is a regular party-goer and is likely to need many dresses over time. A professional stand can cost a great deal of money and isn't even adjustable. You should be able to pick up a home-use, adjustable one for a very reasonable price – there are plenty available on internet auction sites – then you'll have it for future projects.

I use a professional one (affectionately known as Dolly), which will be used for demonstrating exercises throughout this book. As I can draw and pin directly on to 'her', it will be easier for you to understand the principles – and I don't think a live model would take very kindly to such treatment.

Dress stand

Getting Started 13

Steam generator iron

Your iron

The importance of having a good iron cannot be stressed enough. Many a good gown has been ruined by an iron discharging its scaly contents all over lovely, pristine silk.

Whereas professional steam-generated irons were very expensive in the past, they are becoming increasingly affordable. I recently saw one on a home shopping channel for a very reasonable price. A steam generator iron makes the steam in a separate tank so it is very 'dry', cutting down the chance of wetting your fabrics. Iron shields, made from heat-resistant plastic that fits onto the sole plate of your iron, are also helpful. They are very inexpensive and prevent sticking with even the most delicate fabrics.

You also need a sturdy ironing board with a very clean cover. I buy a new cover for each dress I make, but this is probably a bit extreme. At the very least, buy a white or natural cover as coloured ones can bleed onto your fabrics. A sleeve board – a small ironing board for pressing sleeves that fits onto your table or board – is also very useful for pressing darts open as well as getting into tight corners.

Always do a test strip for each new fabric to get the settings on your iron just right. You want the iron and steam to be just hot enough to press the seams flat, but not so hot that the fabric shrinks.

Scissors

Every budding seamstress needs a good pair of scissors or tailoring shears. Make sure they are sharp and you only use them on fabric. Buy the best ones you can afford so they last for years. Mine were purchased over 15 years ago and they are still going strong!

Scissors

Calico (unbleached muslin or quilter's cotton)

Metre rule

Here is a list of other pieces of equipment you will need (you may have most of these already):

- Pins
- Marker pens
- Metre rule or long straight edge
- Designer's square – used as a set square and for adding seam allowances
- Tailor's chalk
- Tape measure
- Rouleau hook (this will be explained later – see page 44)
- Sketchpad and pencils
- Seam ripper
- Small fabric snips
- Spirit level (not essential, but can be handy if you don't have a good eye for lining up straight edges)
- Pattern paper or large sheets of brown paper.

Fabrics

You will also need a good supply of medium-weight calico (known as unbleached muslin or quilter's cotton in the U.S.). This will be used for our practice exercises: to make a body block (a pattern moulded to your body) and a toile (a mock-up of the actual dress that will be unpicked later to form the pattern for the final dress). Buy about 11 yards (10 metres) or so. It is fairly inexpensive and it's best to make mistakes at this price.

Tailor's chalk

Seam ripper

Rouleau hook

Tape measure

Pins

Fabric snips

Sewing Techniques

This section features simple sewing techniques that are not only essential for making your dress, but are fundamental to nearly all sewing projects you encounter. Get them right now, and everything else later will seem easy.

Sewing a Straight Seam

This is not as straightforward as it sounds. There are several things to consider before you even touch your sewing machine.

Consider the type of fabric you are using. Thicker fabrics like calico need a different tension setting and needle size to very fine silk. Refer to the instructions that came with your machine; they will explain the different tension, pressure and needles used for different fabric weights. Every manufacturer and machine uses slightly different settings.

Make sure you use the right thread type for individual fabrics. A general, multi-purpose thread will be fine for your practice pieces, body block and toile; but you need specific thread types for different weights of fabric.

Do a test run on long strips of waste fabric or calico. This is not only good practice, but tests whether your machine tension is set up correctly.

Let's start to sew!

1 The recommended seam allowance throughout this book is ⅝ in (1.5cm). Seam allowance is the distance that we sew in from the side edge of the garment pieces. There should be markings on the plate of your machine but, to make it easier to begin with, stick a piece of coloured tape to the base plate ⅝ in (1.5cm) from the needle. We will call this the marker.

2 Position your fabric strips with the 'right sides' together and the edges lined up. The 'right side' of the fabric is the side that faces out on your finished garment. With patterned fabrics, for example, this will be the clear, brightly coloured side.

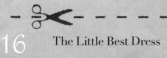

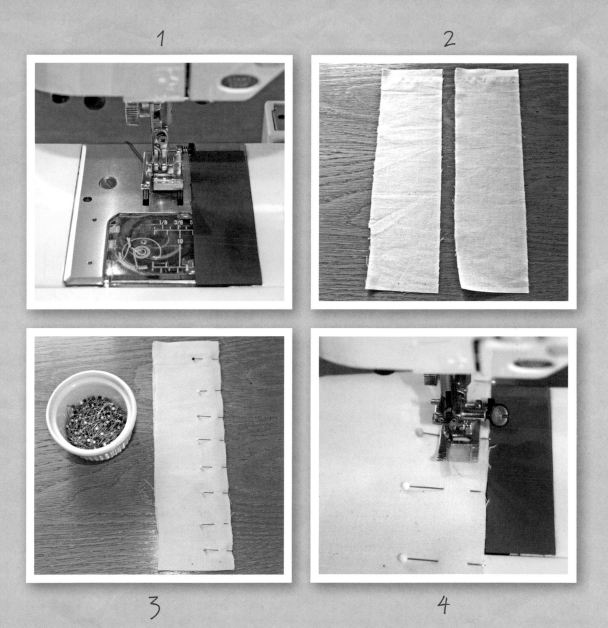

1

2

3

4

3 Pin the strips together at right angles to the stitching line about every 2in (5cm) or so. You can sew quite happily along the stitching line without removing the pins. This speeds up stitching, as it eliminates the need for tacking.

4 Place the pinned strips under the needle, lining the edge up with the marker.

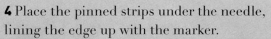

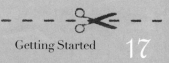

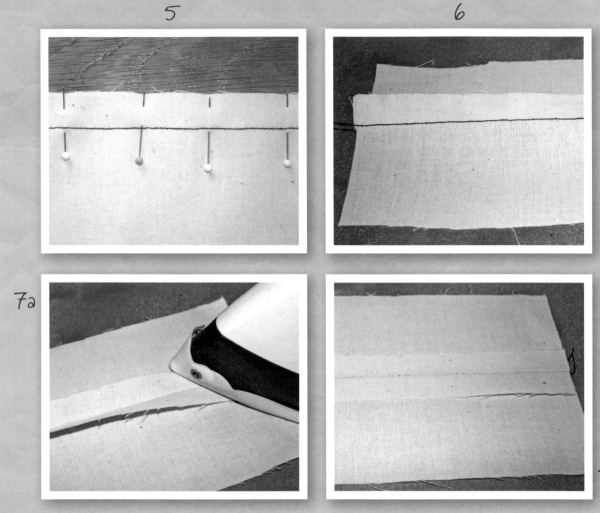

5 Start stitching slowly, going forwards by two or three stitches, then push the reverse button and sew the same backwards. This will make a 'lock stitch' so that the seam does not come undone.

6 Now slowly stitch a straight line, keeping the edges of the fabric running along the marker so that you are stitching ⅝in (1.5cm) in from the edge. When you get to the end of the seam, sew back two or three stitches and forward two or three stitches, just as at the beginning of the seam. This will lock off the end of the seam.

7 Open up the seam allowance and press flat (**7a**). Now, stand back and admire your own work (**7b**). Well done you!

Do a few more strips in the same way, it is a good idea to speed up a little each time until you are confident that you can sew an accurate, straight seam.

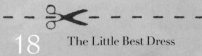

Sewing Around Curves

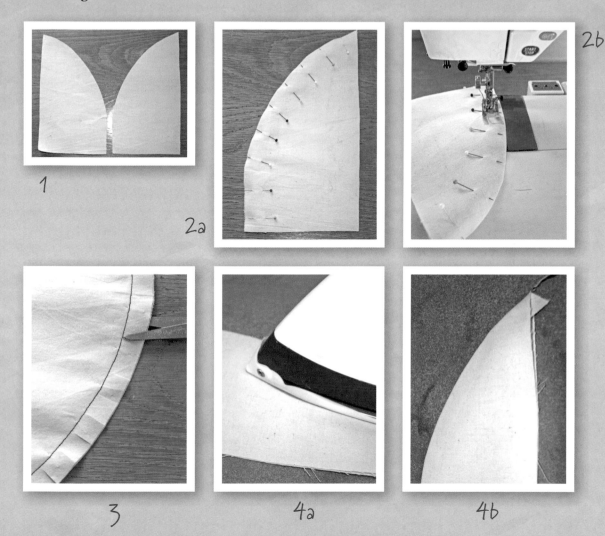

1

2a

2b

3

4a

4b

Two curves facing the same way

These can be sewn in just the same way as straight seams, keeping the edge of the fabric against the marker as you move carefully around.

1 To practise this method, cut out two identical pieces of calico: right angles joined by a curve.

2 Pin together (**2a**), and then sew (**2b**).

3 Using your sharp scissors, snip into the seam allowance to within ¹⁄₁₆in (2mm) of the stitching line, every 2in (5cm) or so. This process is called 'notching', and we will be referring to it on a number of occasions during the book.

4 Turn right sides out and press (**4a**). The seam should be smooth with no sharp angles (**4b**).

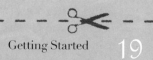

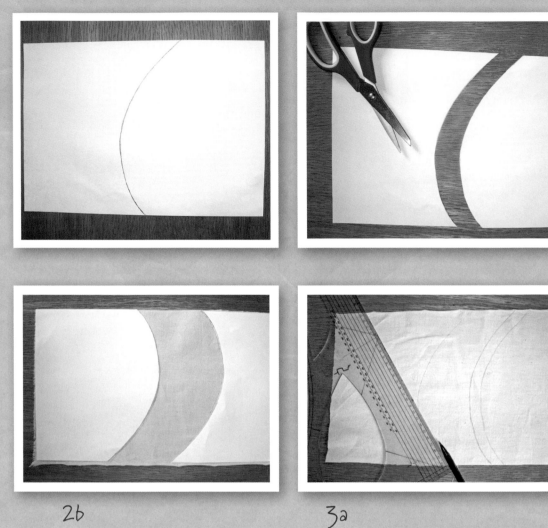

1

2a

2b

3a

One curve in and one curve out

You may want to sew a curved seam into a flat piece of fabric, such as sewing a skirt onto a curved bodice seam.

It is important to note that the stitching line should be ⅝in (1.5cm) in from the edge of your fabric. This is the line that you have to match when sewing the two pieces together, rather than the edge of the fabric.

Let me show you.

1 Begin by drawing a gentle curve on a piece of paper.

2 Cut along the line (**2a**) and lay it out on your piece of calico; trace around the pattern (**2b**) and mark the fabric.

3 Using your designer's set square, add a seam allowance of ⅝in (1.5cm) to the curved edges (**3a** and **3b**).

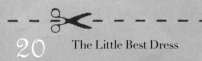

3b

4

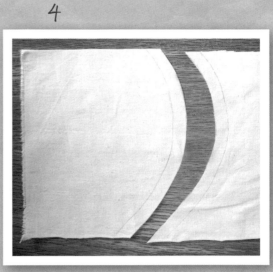

5a

5b

6

4 Now cut out the pattern pieces.

5 Notch (snip into it as a marker) the edge of the pieces on the stitching line, then fold in half and notch the centre line in the seam allowance on both (**5a** and **5b**).

6 With the right sides together, match up the notches and pin at right angles to the seam line.

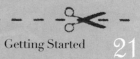

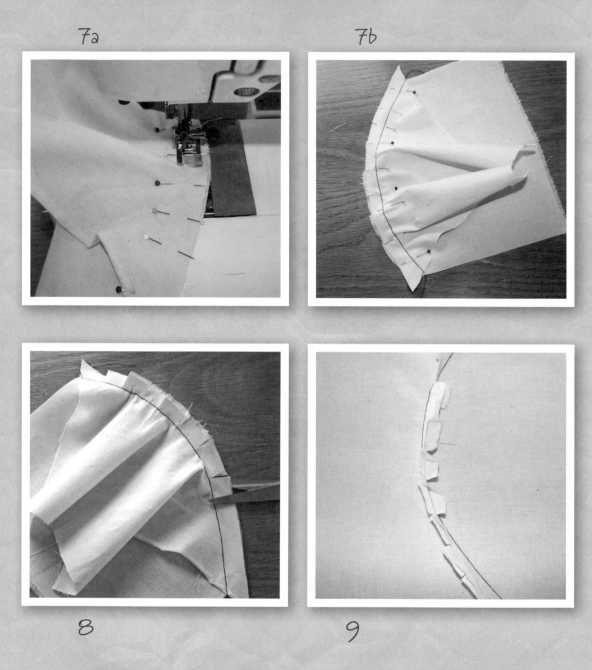

7 Now stitch with your machine, keeping the edge of your fabric along the marker; ease the fabric together as you progress (**7a** and **7b**).

8 Snip into the seam allowance, almost down to the stitching line as we did before, about 2in (5cm) apart.

9 Open out the curved pieces and smooth them flat with your hand.

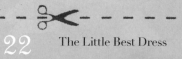

10a

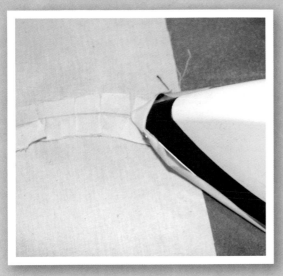

10b

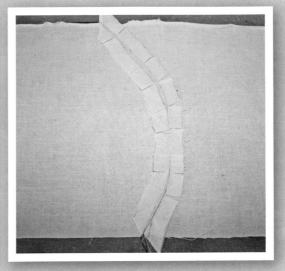

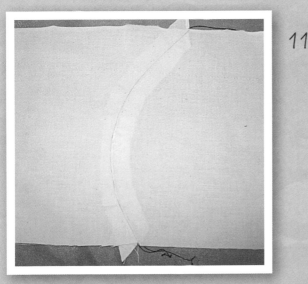

11

10 Press the seam open so that the fabric lies flat with a curved seam (**10a** and **10b**).

11 Now turn over to the 'right side' of the fabric and sing yourself praise.

Repeat a few more times, using curves of different sizes, until you feel confident and understand the principle of the technique.

Once you have mastered straight and curved seams, you can pretty much sew anything. It's only a matter of practice and confidence. All of the seams described in this book will be straight, curved or a combination of both.

Gathers and Pleats

Practise these techniques as many times as you can – you will be using them a lot when making your dresses.

When you practise gathering, you need to gather at a ratio of about three to one, which means that the material to be gathered should be about three times as long as the seam that it will be gathered to. As you progress, you can gradually gather more and more fabric at higher and higher ratios. When I'm gathering organza or chiffon for a skirt, I often use a ten-to-one ratio or even more!

There are three different methods for sewing gathers and pleats (**A**) – which one you choose is up to you.

THREE METHODS OF GATHERING
As you can see, there isn't a great deal of difference between the three finished gathering methods. The choice is up to you. From top: method 1, method 2, method 3.

For any of the methods, take two lengths of fabric, one three times longer than the other at the edge to be gathered. It is much easier to finish the gathering and joining edges by overlocking (serging) or overcasting before you start to sew (**B**).

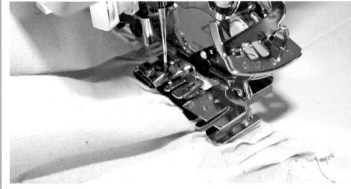

Method 1

1 I use this method for gathering very long pieces of trim; for example, if I'm making a frill around the bottom of a gathered or full circle skirt. All machine manufacturers that I know of produce a ruffle (gathering) foot attachment for their machines, even for very old models. I remember my grandma having one for her old treadle Singer machine. The foot looks about the same for all models.

I know it looks a little daunting if you haven't seen one of these before, but don't be put off: they are incredibly easy to use, and are well worth the cost for the time they save alone.

2 Follow the manufacturer's instructions, as they all differ slightly. Run the fabric to be gathered right side down through the attachment, and the fabric to gather on to right side up under the attachment. This way you can gather and stitch the pieces together in one operation.

3 Press the seam line towards the non-gathered fabric.

4 How easy was that? Try adjusting the stitch length and the settings on your attachment and see what happens. I often use organza ribbon through my gathering foot to create nice edgings and trims.

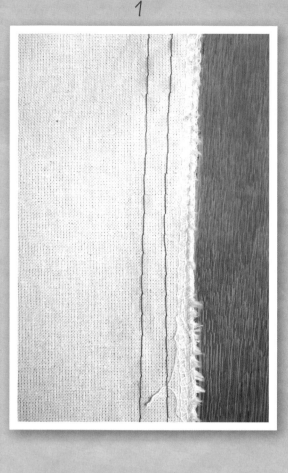

1

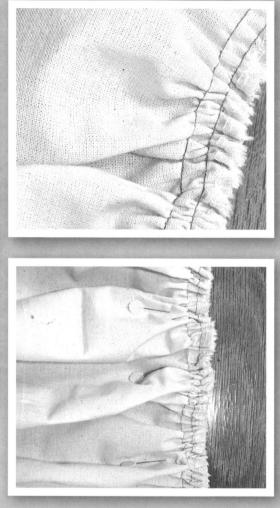

2

3

Method 2

I use this method for sleeve heads and other areas where I want a very precise ratio of gather.

1 Starting with your three-to-one ratio fabrics again, take the long piece first. Set the stitch length on your machine to the longest that it will go and run two lines of stitching along the gathering edge, about ½in (1cm) apart. Don't worry if the stitching lines go over your seam allowance, as we are going to take out the stitching later.

2 Hold the top two threads at one side, and make a gather by sliding the fabric between your thumb and forefinger towards the middle of the work.

3 Gather evenly so that the gathered fabric is the same length as the length of the non-gathered fabric. With right sides together, pin the two pieces together along the seam.

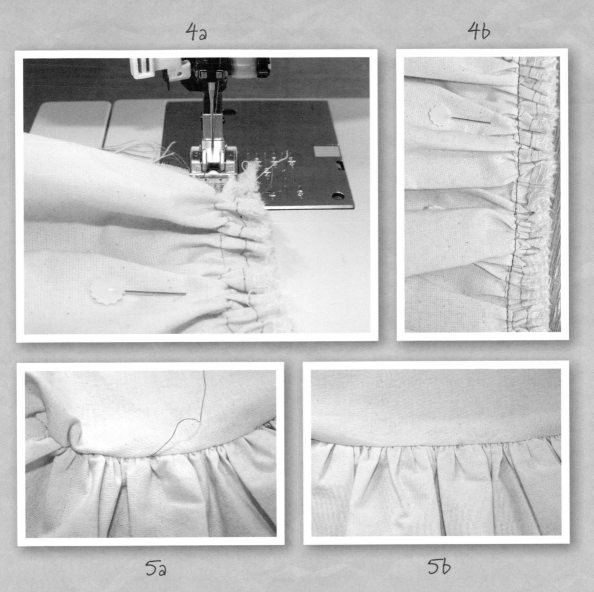

4a

4b

5a

5b

4 Stitch with a ⅝ in (1.5cm) seam allowance (**4a** and **4b**).

5 Any gathering threads that show on the right side of the work can easily be pulled out (**5a**).

Press, as we did before (**5b**).

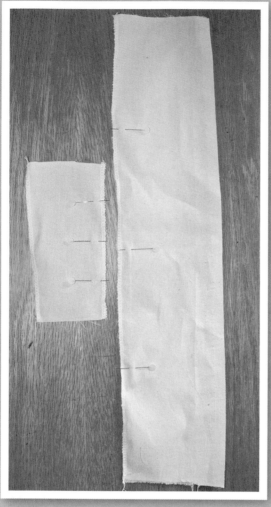

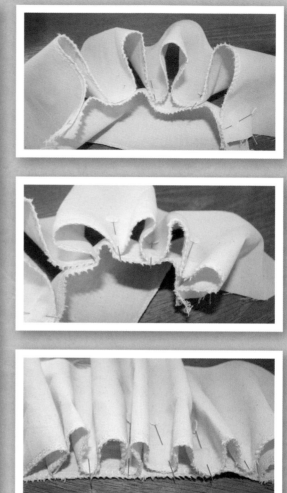

Method 3

This method can be used for evenly placed pleats and gathers. I tend to use this method when I'm attaching a very full gathered skirt to a bodice, or when I need a gather ratio of more than four to one.

1 Divide both pieces of fabric into four equal sections and mark with pins.

2 With right sides together, match up the pins on both pieces of fabric. Pin through both pieces at the match points. Remove the marking pins.

3 Taking one section of top and bottom fabric at a time, divide the area between the pins again and pin.

4 Repeat this between each set of pins. If we were using much longer lengths of fabric, we would carry on this way, dividing each section in half, until we have easy-to-manage lengths of fabric in between the pin markers.

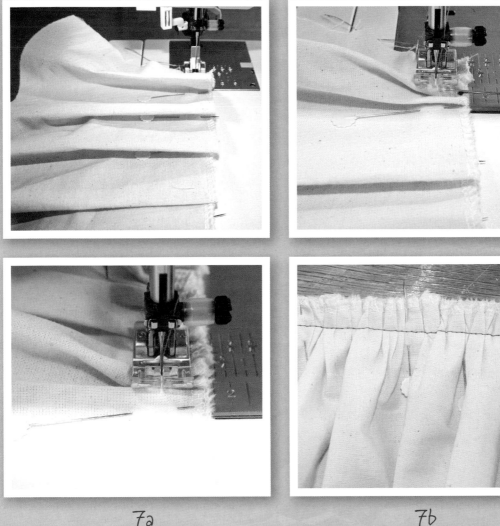

5 With the fabric to be gathered on the top, place the seam under the presser foot and lay the resulting pleats towards you.

At this stage, you could just stitch the seam allowance and you would have perfectly balanced pleats. You can fold them towards you or away from you, depending on which way you want the pleats to lie.

6 Using a fine screwdriver or a seam ripper, gather the top fabric evenly between the pin markers as you stitch, dealing with the work section by section.

7 Push the top fabric under the foot as you go, being careful not to let the needle come down on the seam ripper – or worse, your finger! (**7a** and **7b**)

Take out the pins and press as before.

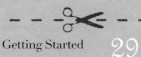

Darts

Darts are a way of reducing or suppressing fabric when you don't want to shape a garment using full seams. They can be either straight or curved. The classic use of darts is at the waist-to-hip suppression on skirts and trousers or the bust-to-waist, shoulder-to-bust, or hip-to-waist-to-bust-to-shoulder suppression on dresses. Some darts, like waist-to-hip or shoulder-to-bust, can be stitched in a single run. Others, like bust-to-waist-to-hip, need more than one stitching run.

We always stitch from the fullest part of the suppression before 'running off' at the smallest part. Don't worry if this sounds a bit confusing, it will become clearer in the next exercise.

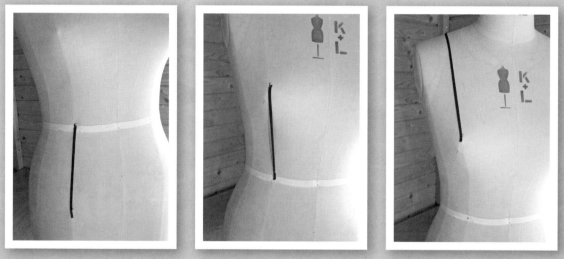

WAIST-TO-HIP   BUST-TO-WAIST   SHOULDER-TO-BUST

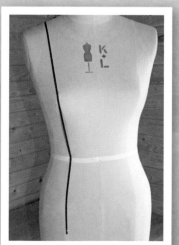

SHOULDER-
TO-BUST-TO-
WAIST-TO-HIP

BUST-TO-
WAIST-TO-HIP

A single-run dart

1 Take a square of calico and rule a line down the centre until you reach about the middle of the fabric.

2 Now measure about 1¼ in (3cm) either side of the centre line at the top end of the fabric and make a mark.

3 Snip these marks and draw a line from the snip to the marked point on the centre.

4 Fold fabric in half along the centre line.

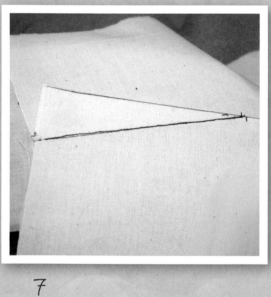

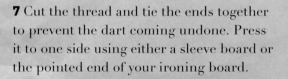

5 Matching up the snips, stitch along your marked line from the top edge to the middle.

6 Be sure to 'run off' the stitching at the end of the dart by letting the machine sew a few stitches beyond the edge of the fabric.

7 Cut the thread and tie the ends together to prevent the dart coming undone. Press it to one side using either a sleeve board or the pointed end of your ironing board.

8 Flip over to reveal the 'right side' of the fabric with a finished dart.

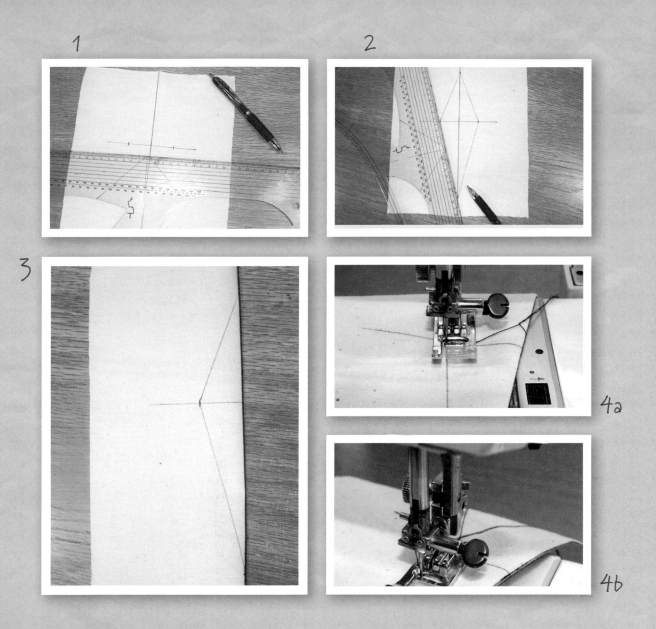

A multiple-dart run

1 Take a square of calico and rule a line down the centre, as we did with the single-dart run (see page 31). Place a mark halfway down this line. Now, using your designer's square, draw a line at right angles to the centre line that runs about 1¼ in (3cm) either side of the centre line.

2 Draw a dot on the centre line about 1½ in (4cm) down from the top of the fabric and 1½ in (4cm) up from the bottom. Connect the dots to mark the dart.

3 Fold fabric in half along the centre line.

4 Stitch along the dart lines – first from the centre to the top running off at the narrowest point (**4a**), and then down from the centre to the bottom (**4b**).

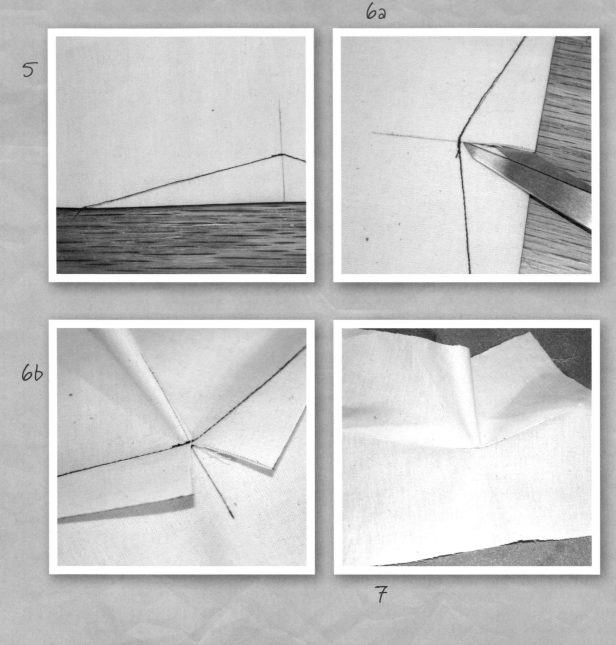

5 Run off the stitching as we did before.

6 Snip into the centre of the dart (**6a**) and press to one side (**6b**).

7 Turn the fabric over to the 'right side' to see your finished double dart.

Oh, how clever you are!

Seam Finishes

Seams are rarely finished off in couture sewing, mostly edges are 'bagged' inside the lining. You may, however, wish to neaten and finish off the seams just in case someone gets a glimpse inside.

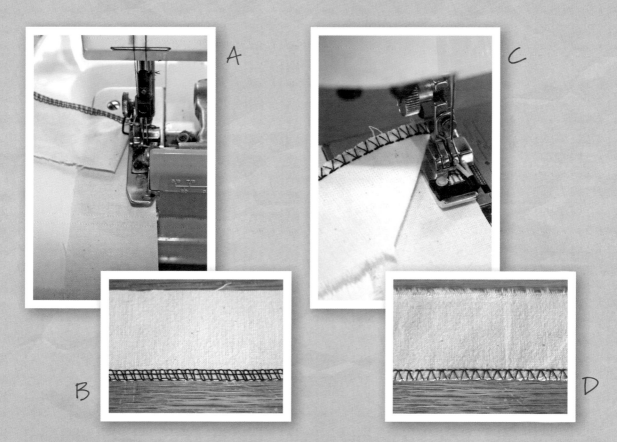

Overlocked edges

Overlockers are the neatest way to finish off a rough edge. They use either three or four threads that bind off the edge of the fabric, removing the rough edges as you sew (**A**).

When overlocking, be careful not to trim off too much edge fabric as this can cut into your seam allowance and alter the size of the finished garment (**B**).

Overcasting

If you don't have access to an overlocker, you can use the zigzag setting on your machine with an overcast foot – see the instruction manual for guidance (**C**).

This is not as neat as an overlocked edge, but it's quite acceptable for the occasional straight seam (**D**).

Hems

A badly turned hem can ruin a beautiful dress. Think of it as wearing hoop earrings with a classic Dior evening gown. This section looks at simple, but very effective, methods of hem finishing.

The traditional hem

The turned-up and then hand- or machine-stitched hem is by far the easiest one to get wrong. You can often see the pressing line on the 'right side', and any visible stitches or puckers will stand out like a sore thumb. Here are some pleasant alternatives.

The bagged-in hem

The bagged-in hem (below) is probably the simplest hemline finish. It's made by cutting out a lining the same length as the skirt, stitching around the hem and turning it through before sewing the skirt to the bodice. This method hides all the seam edges but adds bulk to the finished garment. It also works well on both full or straight skirts, and for either short or long designs.

The roll-turned hem

The roll-turned hem is suitable for linings and underskirts.

Simply press the hem ½in (1cm) to the inside, then turn it down again by ¼in (0.5cm) making a double turn (**1**). Sew on the wrong side, as close to the turned edge as you can (**2**), and then press to form a neat finish.

1

2

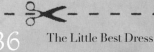

The bias-bound hem

Prepare the bias strips as described on page 38. Sew the unfolded edge to the edge you want to finish using a ½ in (1cm) seam allowance. Now turn the folded edge of the bias strip to the inside and hand-sew in place along the stitching line to bind the edge (**1**, **2**, **3**, **4** and **5**).

This is a very useful technique for finishing all sorts of edges, hems, armholes, necklines and so on. As the strip is cut on the bias or cross grain, it will stretch and shrink easily and works well with curved seams (**6**).

The bias-bagged hem

This is a really nice hem finish. It adds weight and body to a hem line and, as there is a seam line at the edge rather than a fold, it is very neat. It can be used on any shaped hem and is very useful for curved hems like full circle skirts. There is some hand sewing required so it is sensible to practise many times to develop confidence.

To make bias strips

You can buy bias binding in cotton and satin, but it looks much nicer if you make it from the main fabric of your garment – and it's also very easy to do.

1 Lay out your fabric and rule 2in (5cm) lines at 45-degree angles across the fabric.

2 Cut along lines, lay the ends of two strips together at right angles and stitch. Repeat for other pieces, stitching together to make one long strip, and then press (**2a** and **2b**).

3 Fold width ways by ½in (1cm) and press. This will be the edge that you hand sew in place.

4 Next you need to take a practice strip of fabric about 4in (10cm) wide. With the 'right sides' together, stitch the unpressed edge of the bias strip to the edge of the practice piece using a ½in (1cm) seam allowance (**4a–4d**).

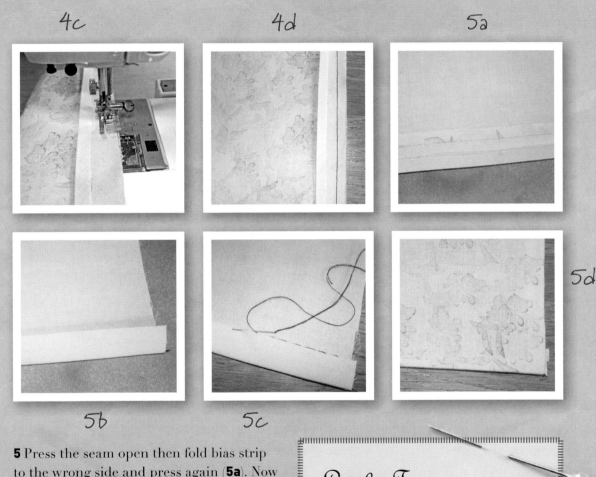

4c

4d

5a

5b

5c

5d

5 Press the seam open then fold bias strip to the wrong side and press again (**5a**). Now hand sew in place, catching just one thread on the main fabric with each stitch (**5b–5d**).

Press again.

Little Tip

The right side of a fabric is the one that will face outwards on your finished garment. With patterned fabrics, for example, this will be the clear, brightly coloured side.

Fastenings

In much the same way as hems, badly inserted fastenings can spoil otherwise elegant and beautifully finished garments. Paying attention to detail pays off! This section explores a number of different fastenings – from zips to rouleau loops.

Zips

The easiest and best-looking fastening of all is the concealed or invisible zip. From the outside it looks just like another seam, but concealed zips are slightly different from normal zips, as the slider is on the opposite side.

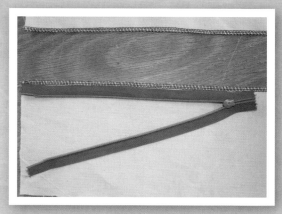

1

To insert an invisible zip

As with many other sewing techniques in this book, this process is much simpler than it seems. As soon as you have added an invisible zip, you will get the principle and never use a normal zip again.

Purchase a few 8 or 10in (20 or 25cm) concealed zips from your local sewing shop, remembering that they are different from normal zips.

1 Take two pieces of scrap fabric and place onto the table with the 'right sides' facing up. Now undo the zip. The right side (front) actually looks more like the wrong side (back) of the zip.

With the wrong side facing up, open the zip fully and place the right-hand tape onto the left piece of fabric – make sure the end of the tape is at the top of the fabric.

You will find that you can roll open the 'teeth' on the wrong side of the zip just by holding the tape flat to the fabric with your right hand, and rolling the teeth to the left. We are going to sew in this crease line.

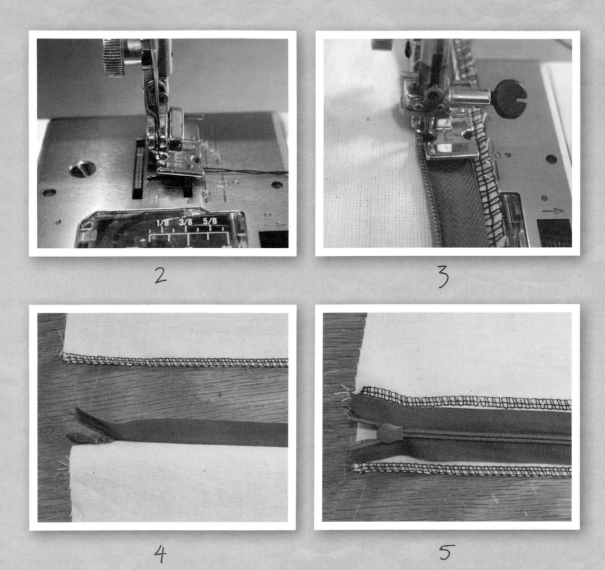

2

3

4

5

2 Attach the zipper foot to your machine (see manufacturer's instructions) so that the needle is on the left side of the foot.

3 With the edge of the zipper tape ¼in (0.5cm) in from the edge of the fabric, roll open the 'teeth' slightly. Now, stitching in the crease line, sew down to about ⅝in (1.5cm) from the 'stop staple' at the bottom of the zip. Remember to do a lock stitch at the start and end.

4 Close the zip. Now tuck the seam under, folding the zipper tape to the 'wrong side' of the fabric. Place it alongside the second piece of fabric and flip it over so that the fabric right sides are together.

5 Undo the zip.

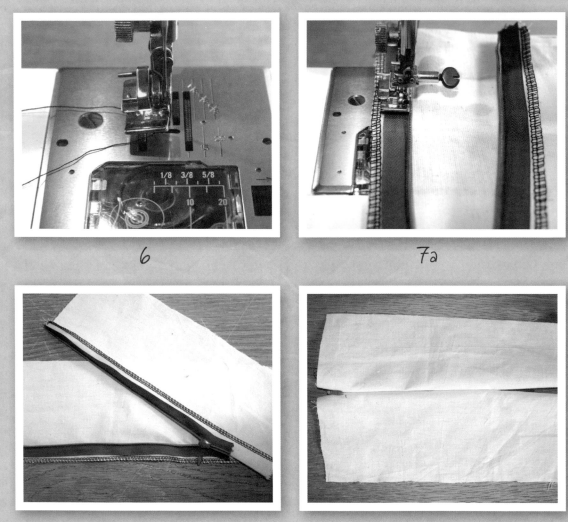

6

7a

7b

8

6 Move the zipper foot so that the needle is on the right-hand side of the foot.

7 Sew down the zipper tape, just as you did for the first side (see page 41), making sure that you stop ¾ in (2cm) from the 'stop staple' at the bottom of the zip (**7a** and **7b**).

8 Open up the work so that the 'right side' is facing up. Now do up the zip so that it looks like a normal seam.

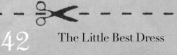

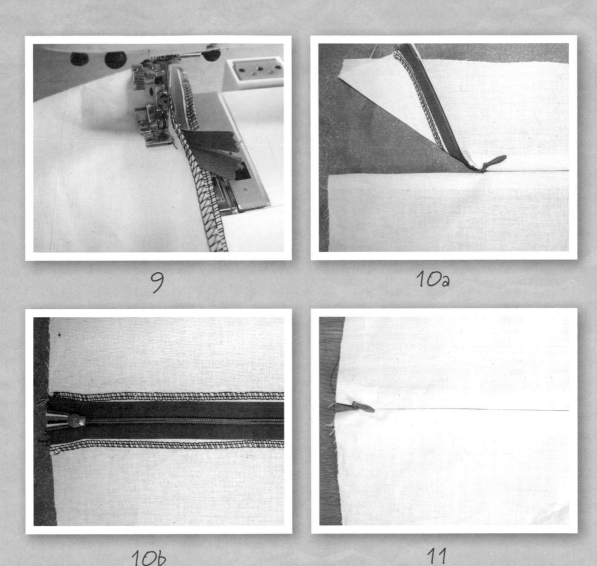

9

10a

10b

11

9 Fold all of the fabric right sides together and, leaving the zipper foot in the same position, stitch down from where the stitching line stops.

Be very careful not to catch the zipper tape by folding the zip in half and pulling it slightly out of the way as you stitch down.

10 Press the seam open on the wrong side of the fabric and press over the zip on the right side (**10a** and **10b**).

11 Insert several zips using this very same technique until you're confident with the entire procedure.

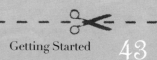

Buttons and Rouleau Loops

Buttons and loops create a very nice effect, especially when you place the buttons close together. You can place a row of buttons and loops down the back of a dress, a few on a cuff or one as a back neck fastening.

A rouleau is a thin strip of bias-cut fabric that is seamed down one side, then turned through to make a 'tube'. These are often used as loops for buttons or lacing, as well as for straps on tops, dresses and lingerie.

1

2

3

4

How to make rouleau loops

1 Lay out your fabric and mark bias strips of ¾ in (2cm). Cut out the strips then, working each one in turn, fold in half along the width. Stitch in from the folded edge using a ¼ in (0.5cm) seam allowance.

2 Using a rouleau hook (a thin length of wire with a latch-hook at one end), push the hook end inside the rouleau and grab the top end of the rouleau.

3 Very slowly and carefully pull through by turning the rouleau right side out.

4 Take the required button size and then measure around the circumference. Add 1¼ in (3cm) to this figure and you will have the precise measurement for cutting your rouleau loops.

5 Cut two strips of waste fabric to a width of 4in (10cm). Notch markings down one side, ⅝in (1.5cm) apart.

6 Fold one rouleau loop in half, line up the raw edges with the edge of your fabric (right side up) on the notched mark and pin them into place. When all the loops are in position, run a line of stitching ½in (1cm) in from the edge of the fabric to secure.

7 Remove the pins. Place the second strip of fabric over the first with the 'right sides' together. This is called the 'facing' – it traps all of the loops in between the two layers of fabric.

8 Stitch down the fabric using a ⅝in (1.5cm) seam allowance.

9 Fold the 'facing' around to the back of the work, exposing the loops, before pressing flat.

10 'Face' a second strip of fabric – as in the previous step, but without the rouleau loops – and press. Lay the looped and plain pieces side-by-side and sew on the buttons to correspond with the loops.

How to make covered buttons

There are several different types of self-cover buttons on the market and several different ways of covering them; there is no right or wrong way if it works. The method shown here works well for all button sizes.

I tend to favour the metal self-cover buttons, as I think they are more durable, but other designers I know swear by the plastic kind. It's a good idea to try both and see which you prefer.

1 Cut a circle out of your chosen fabric about a third bigger than the button.

2 Thread a needle with any thread and sew a running stitch around the fabric circle, a little way in from the edge.

3 Place the dome, or front, of the button face down on the wrong side of the fabric (**3a**) and pull the gathering thread up (**3b**).

4 Snap the back of the button on to the front, leaving the thread hanging out.

5 Snip off the thread and the job is done!

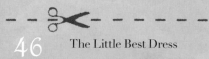

Lacing

Lacing up the back of a corset or basque top can be a very effective technique. It allows a little ease for fitting a garment, as it can be either laced looser or tighter depending on the wearer.

Lacing works best on boned garments, but is occasionally used for fastening skirts or cuffs. You need to make either holes or eyelets in a fabric in order to thread the lacing through; there are several ways to do this. Eyelets and suitable tools to apply them directly to fabric can be purchased from haberdashery stores. I tend not to use this method, as it often splits the fabric and the holes can fray.

You can also buy eyelet tape, which has strong eyelet holes already made. It's quite effective on corsets, but I would only use this method if the tape isn't going to show on the finished garment.

The third, and my preferred method of lacing, is to use rouleau loops and ribbon or lacing cord.

Apply the loops, but don't make them as long as you did in the previous exercise. Ensure that the loops are evenly spaced and that you have the same number on both sides. Lace up with cord or ribbon (**A** and **B**).

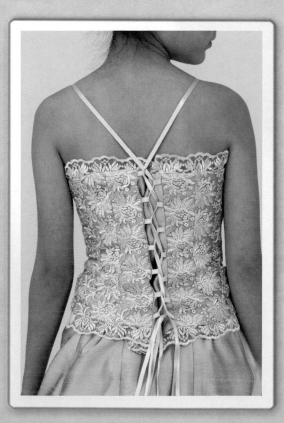

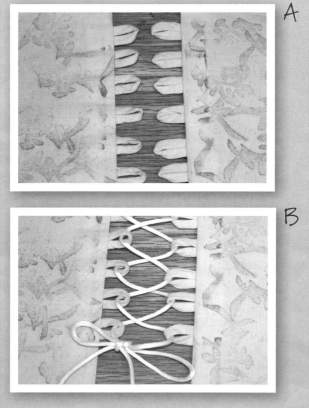

A

B

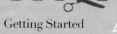

Net Underskirts

There is nothing nicer to a little girl than layers and layers of prettiness. Make one of these and I'm sure she'll be delighted!

To start with, you need to take a few measurements:

- Hip
- Waist to hip
- Hip to floor (or the desired length of the underskirt)

1 Take a rectangle of lining fabric that is twice the hip measurement in length, and the waist-to-hip measurement plus 1in (2.5cm) in width. Overlock or overcast the fabric all the way around.

2 Fold in one of the long edges by ¾in (2cm) and press.

Little Tip

The underskirts make a fabulous addition to any dressing-up box. Make them with even more layers for a more dramatic look and perhaps try making every layer a different colour!

1

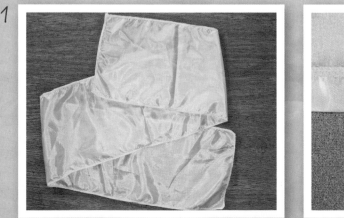

2

3 Stitch the folded fabric ⅝in (1.5cm) in from the edge to form a channel for the waist elastic.

4 Now take a length of dress net that is four times the length of the lining fabric by twice the hip-to-floor length (so that when you fold it you end up with two layers). Fold the net in half lengthways and press the crease.

Next, using your preferred method of gathering (see page 24), gather up the net on the fold so that it fits the length of the lining fabric. I have used my gathering foot.

5 Cut the same amount of dress net again. Fold and gather in the same way so that you end up with four layers of gathered net in total.

6 Lay the unfolded edge of the lining under the machine foot with the folded edge on the right-hand side and the overlocked edge under the foot.

Place the gathered edges of both pieces of net together and lap them over the overlocked lining under the machine foot (this sounds harder than it is).

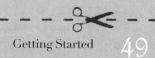

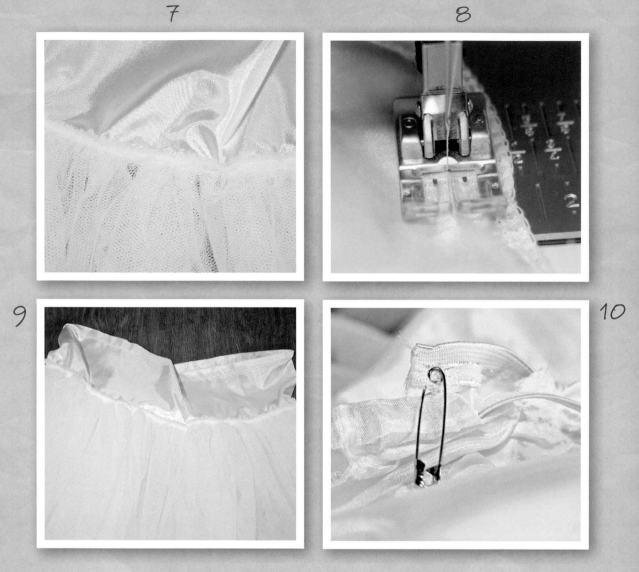

7 Set your machine to a short and wide zigzag stitch. Stitch over the lapped seam, making sure that the lining stays in line with the left-hand side of the foot, and the net stays in line with the right-hand side of the foot. Using the zigzag stitch creates a very flat seam that will not scratch your princess and will not show through the top fabric of the dress.

8 With right sides of the lining together, sew down the back seam of the lining only; start just after the elastic opening and stop where the net joins the lining.

9 Turn through to the right side.

10 Cut a piece of elastic slightly smaller than the waist measurement. Thread it through the lining opening; I find a safety pin helps with this.

11

12a

12b

12c

11 Tie the elastic off firmly and the underskirt is nearly ready to be worn!

12 Now, to finish off the hem neatly, zigzag a length of fine satin ribbon close to the hem edge on the top layer of the underskirt (**12a** and **12b**).

I think that every little best dress needs a real couture finish so I've satin-edged all four layers! (**12c**).

Fabric Flowers

A corsage over one shoulder or a few rosebuds at the hip can look stunning, and are surprisingly easy to make. Use the same fabric as the gown for a subtle approach, or contrasting tones for impact. Chiffon and organza flowers add a more delicate look.

Simple fabric roses
Use strips of fabric. Mine was 18in (45cm) long and 4in (10cm) wide.

1 Fold the strip in half widthways and finish the long edge. Fold the unfinished edge down to the overlocked edge (**1a**). Stitch along the overlocked edge, gathering as you go (**1b**). Near the end of the seam, fold in the other raw edge. Sew to the end (**1c**).

1a

1b

1c

**FABRIC ROSE
AND ROSEBUD**

2a

2b

2 Thread a needle with double thread. Starting from one end roll up the fabric, overlocking at the bottom, and stitch in place as you go. You have a rose! (**2a–2c**)

Rosebud
Use a shorter and narrower piece of fabric than for the rose.

3 Overlock the fabric and fold over the ends (**3a**). Gather up the strip, less tightly than for the rose (**3b**).

4 Roll up and finish in exactly the same way as for the rose.

2c

3a

3b

4

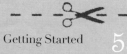

Headdresses

These little headdresses are really pretty, and the 'must-have' accessory for any party dress. Use the flowers and buds that we made on pages 52–53 in the same fabrics as your little dress for that real 'fully coordinated Princess' look.

Alice band

Make a tube of fabric the right width for the band and a little bit longer. Thread the band through; as the fabric is longer than the band, it gathers up nicely. Hold the ends in place with some hot glue. Using the same glue, just stick the flowers in place as you want them. Make sure that the rough ends of the flowers are all hidden. You could even add some leaves or crystals at this point.

Circlet

For the circlet I used some polyester boning from the local haberdashery store, cut to the required length. Cover it in fabric as for the Alice band and glue on the flowers, spacing them evenly.

Comb

The comb is even easier; just glue the flowers to the edge of a hair comb.

Fairy Wings

Every little girl loves fairy wings – the prettier the better. Make these to match any of the dresses in this book and watch as your princess flutters off into a fantasy world!

You will need:

- ■ Some millinery wire
- ■ Clear-drying glue
- ■ Crushed crystal organza (or any transparent fine fabric)
- ■ Some elastic
- ■ Small length of polyester boning (optional)

1 The proportions are important for wings. Measure from the nape of the neck to the waist, and draw a square with sides of this measurement onto a large piece of paper.

Using a fine pencil, draw in one side of the wings, making them any shape that you feel is realistic for your fairy. When you're happy with the shape, mark in using a felt-tip pen. Leave a little 'tab', as shown, to stitch the wings together with later.

2 Take a length of millinery wire and, holding it in place with sticky tape, use it to trace around one side of your wing shape, bending the wire as you go.

Repeat for the second side.

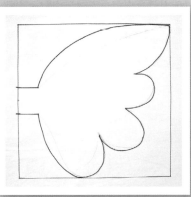

1

2

3 Spread some clear-drying glue all over one side of the wire on both wings. Lay the wings, glue side down, onto your transparent wing fabric.

4 Spread more glue carefully on the upper side of the wire. Now lay another piece of your fabric over the top to cover the wings.

Leave until the glue is completely dry, preferably overnight. If you need your wings sooner, a hairdryer can speed up the drying time.

5 Set your sewing machine to a fine zigzag with a short stitch (refer to the manufacturer's instructions). Using an open-toe foot, carefully zigzag over the wire all round your wings.

6 Now cut all round the wings, on the outside of the wire. Cut as close as you can to the stitching but be careful not to cut your stitches.

The Little Best Dress

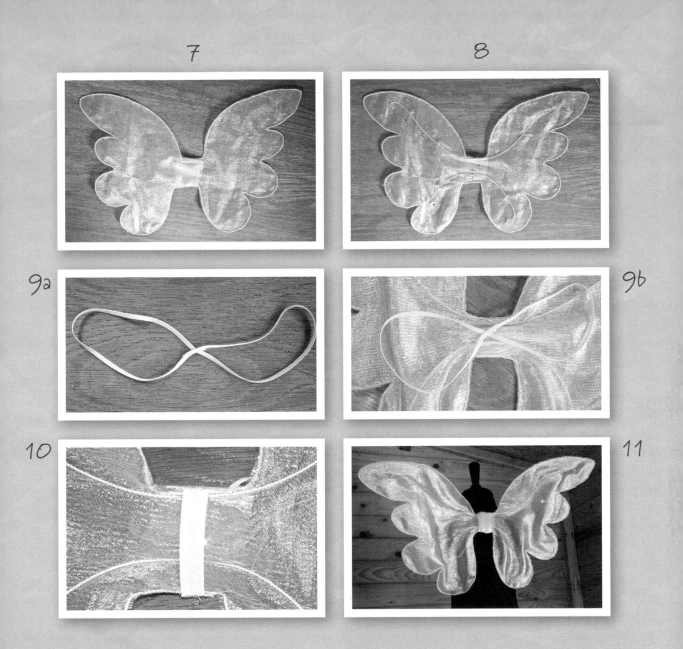

7 Lay one wing over the other at the centre to reveal the shape of your fabulous wings!

8 Cut two pieces of wire to make the veins. Pin in place and zigzag stitch as before.

9 Take a length of elastic long enough to go round the arms at the shoulders, meeting in the centre of the back. Make a figure of eight and stitch at the centre (**9a** and **9b**).

10 Stitch a small length of polyester boning at the centre back, as shown. Don't worry if you can't find boning, a couple a lengths of your wire will do just as well.

11 Tie a little piece of matching fabric over the boning at the centre back to neaten and cover the join.

And now get ready for your little one to flutter about in her new wings!

Making the Blocks

'A girl should be two things:
classy and fabulous.'

COCO CHANEL

The Body Block

A body block is a fabric rendition of half your princess's exact body shape. It is made using old couture techniques that are actually quite simple to execute. It is very important to get the body block just right, because all the dress patterns in this book will be manipulated from the block that you make.

Follow the instructions very carefully and systematically and you will do just fine.

You will need:

- A tape measure
- A designer's square
- Calico
- Marker pen with a fine tip
- Pins
- Elastic
- A spirit level (not essential, but can be useful if you have difficulty judging a horizontal line by eye)
- A very tight-fitting white t-shirt for your model (buy one or two sizes too small so that it fits very tightly). Fold the t-shirt in half down the centre front matching up the side seams and make a mark at the neckline and at the hemline. Draw a line with your felt-tip pen between these points to mark the centre line (**A**). Do the same down the centre back.

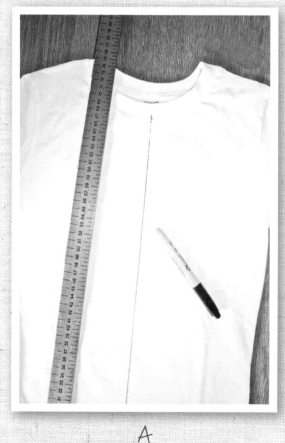

A

You will now need to take seven measurements:

- Chest
- Hips
- Nape of the neck to just below the buttocks
- Bust point to bust point (nipple to nipple)
- Shoulder blade to shoulder blade
- Above shoulder to bust point
- Above shoulder to shoulder blade point.

Write these measurements down carefully.

1 Cut two strips of calico: the width should be one quarter of the chest or hip measurement (the larger of the two), plus 4in (10cm); the length should be the measurement from the nape of the neck to just below the buttocks, plus 4in (10cm). Fold back ⅝in (1.5cm) of fabric down one of the long edges on each piece of calico and press.

2 Now place the two strips on your table, with the turned-in edge on the left piece on the left side and the turned-in edge on the right piece on the right side. Write 'front' on the right-hand piece and 'back' on the left-hand piece.

3 Working with the front piece, measure in from the folded edge by half of the bust-point-to-bust-point measurement and mark the point (**3a**). Do this in a couple of places and draw a line through the points, making sure it is parallel to the folded edge of the fabric (**3b**).

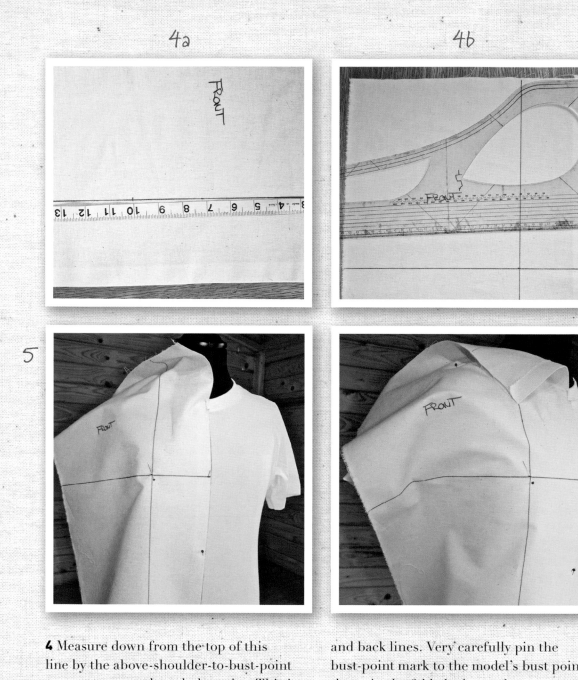

4 Measure down from the top of this line by the above-shoulder-to-bust-point measurement and mark the point. This is the bust point (**4a**). Using the designer's square, draw a line at right angles to the first line, cutting through the bust point mark (**4b**).

5 Your model needs to stand very still and upright, with shoulders back, wearing the tight t-shirt marked with centre-front

and back lines. Very carefully pin the bust-point mark to the model's bust point, then pin the folded edge to the centre line on the t-shirt, keeping the bust line horizontal.

6 With the flat of your hand, smooth the fabric across the hip and pin at the side. Then smooth the fabric up from the bust and pin to just below the shoulder.

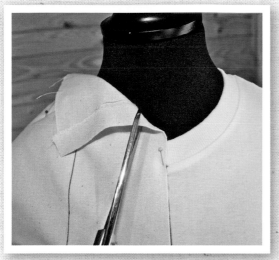

7a

7b

8a

8b

7 We are now going to mark in the neckline with sharp scissors. Being careful not to cut your model, point the scissors upwards, place the scissor point just to the left of the neckline and snip up (**7a**). This will free up some of the fabric, making it sit closer to the body. Continue this method all around the neck to the shoulder seam (**7b**).

8 Now that the block sits close to the neck, mark around the neck shape (**8a**). Cut away the excess fabric. Pin to hold at the neck edge of the shoulder (**8b**).

9

Little Tip

Stand very still and straight for as long as you can and the fit of your dress will be perfect. There will be a lot of pins used so here's a tip a princess client of mine taught me: hide a pin in your hand and if your seamstress sticks you with a pin... you can pretend to stick her back!

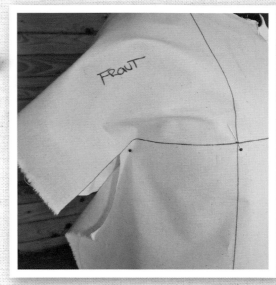

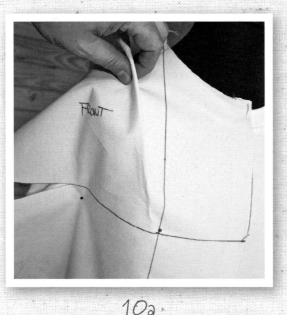

10a

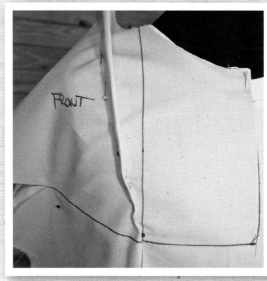

10b

9 We will now insert the shoulder-to-bust-point dart. Cut a line in from the side seam, following the chest line, stopping just before the armhole seam on the t-shirt.

10 Look at the bust line and straighten it so that it runs absolutely horizontal (you may want to use a spirit level). Pin the bust line to the side seam. You will see that you have some excess fabric between the chest and the shoulder. Pinch this excess fabric out to form a dart, about halfway along the shoulder (**10a**). It doesn't matter where this dart falls, as we are going to manipulate the position of it later. Pin along the length of the dart (**10b**).

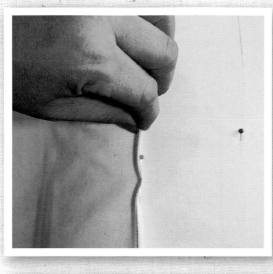

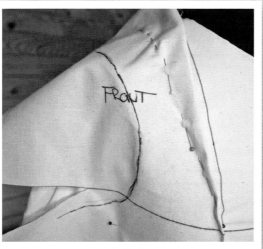

11 We are now going to suppress the waist dart up to the chest and down to the hip. Folding on the line, as we did with the bust dart, pin out the fullness at the waist (**11a**). Pin up to the bust point, then down to the hip. Fit close to the body but be careful not to stretch the t-shirt (**11b**).

Note All we are doing at the moment is making a fabric rendering of the body. Style is not important at this stage. On some children, the waist measurement

may be larger than the chest measurement. It is still important to include the darts, even though they may not look exactly like mine. Just pin out any fullness on the line. For smaller children, don't worry if there is no fabric to pin out. Children do come in all shapes and sizes!

12 Mark around the armhole seam from the edge of the shoulder to the underarm following the seam on the t-shirt (**12a**). Trim away the excess fabric (**12b**).

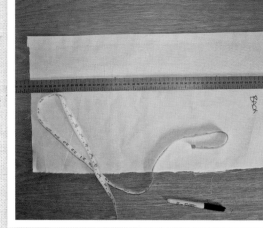

15

13 Mark in both sides of all darts, following the pin lines.

The front block is finished for the time being. We are now going to repeat the process for the back.

14 Take the back piece that we cut earlier. Measure in from the folded edge by the shoulder-blade-to-shoulder-blade measurement and mark the point. Do this in several places and draw a line through the marks, parallel to the folded edge.

15 Measure down the line, from the top, by the above-shoulder-to-shoulder-blade measurement and mark the point. This is the blade point. Using the designer's square, draw a line at right angles to the first line, cutting through the blade point.

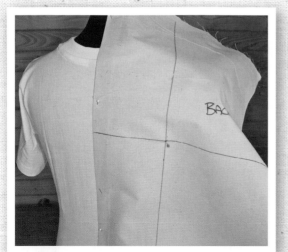

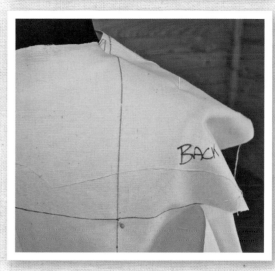

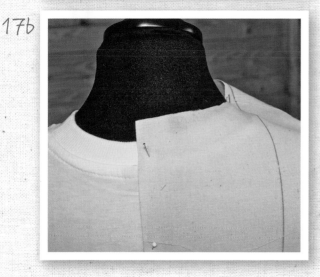

16 With your model standing very straight again, pin the blade point to the shoulder blade and the centre back to the centre-back line on the t-shirt. Place a pin to hold the shoulder line up, ensuring the blade line is absolutely horizontal. Smooth fabric out to the hip and pin at the side seam.

17 Now snip into the back neck as we did for the front (**17a**). Mark the neckline and trim the excess fabric. Pin the fabric at the neck edge of the shoulder (**17b**).

18 Cut in from the side seam along the blade line, stopping close to the armhole seam on the t-shirt.

Pin under the arm, keeping the blade line horizontal. Smooth the fabric upwards and pin out the shoulder dart, as we did for the bust dart. In the case of my block, there was no excess fabric to pin out at the shoulder but don't worry if you have; remember, every body shape is different.

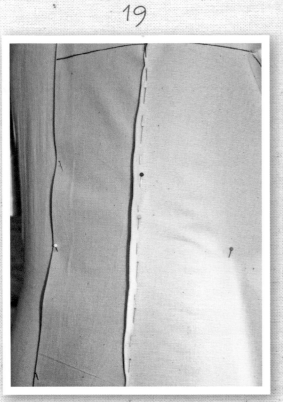

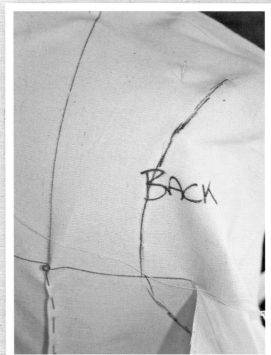

19 Pin out the waist dart up to the blade point and down to the hip, just as we did for the front.

Note For most children, the back dart suppressions will be much larger than the front dart suppressions. This is perfectly normal, so don't worry.

20 Mark the armhole, following the armhole seam on the t-shirt (**20a**).

Cut away the excess fabric (**20b**).

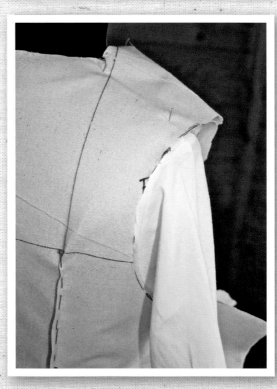

20b

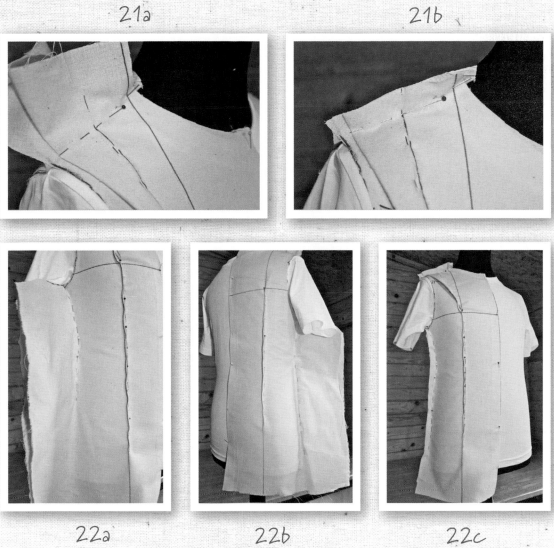

21a

21b

22a

22b

22c

21 Pin in the shoulder line, pinning the back to the front and keeping as close to the shoulder as you can (**21a**).

Trim away the excess fabric (**21b**).

22 With the model's arm bent and slightly out to the side, and the elbow in line with the slope of the shoulder, remove the pins at the hips and the underarm. Pin the side seams in, keeping as close to the body as you can without stretching the t-shirt (**22a** and **22b**).

Cut away the excess fabric (**22c**).

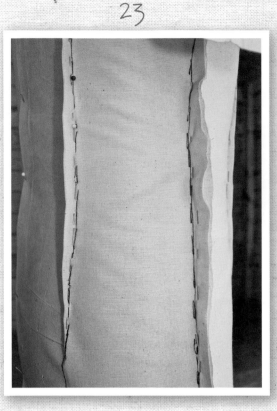

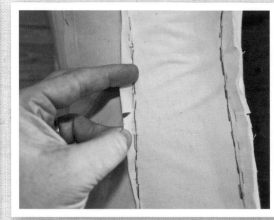

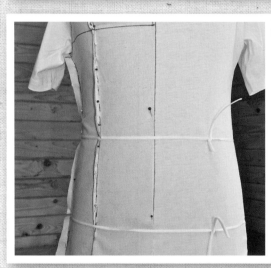

23 Mark in both sides of all darts and the shoulder seam and side seams.

24 Snip into the darts and side seams at the waist line to 'relax' the fabric a little.

25 Tie a length of elastic around the waist and another round the hips (**25a**). Make sure that each piece of elastic is absolutely horizontal and mark the lines around the body block using the elastics as guides. Use a spirit level if you need to (**25b**).

25a

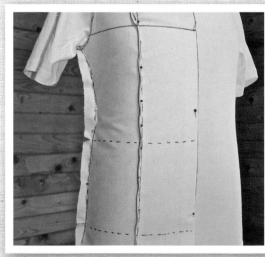

25b

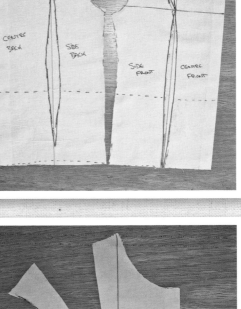

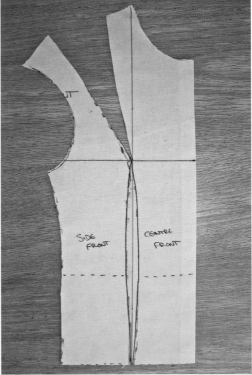

26 Take out all the pins and take the block off the model. Press the calico and lay the pieces out on the table. If you have ever made a purchased pattern, you will begin to recognize the shapes.

27 Cut the pattern pieces along the hip lines. Cut off the side seam allowances and the shoulder seam allowance (we are going to add an accurate seam allowance later).

28 Cut out the v-shaped dart from the shoulder to chest on the front piece.

We are now going to make and fit a full body block from these pattern pieces.

The Full Block

We've made a block that fits one side of your model, so now we need to test it to see if it works as a full block. Again, this stage is very important. It's no good making up a pattern from your block only to find that it doesn't fit later.

FABRI-BASTE

To start with, we are going to transfer the body block on to some pattern paper, or my new favourite 'friend' in the sewing room: Fabri-Baste. This is a non-woven material, similar to interfacing or embroidery stabilizer but much stronger. It is so strong that you can even sew it and, if you make a pattern out if it, it can be used again and again.

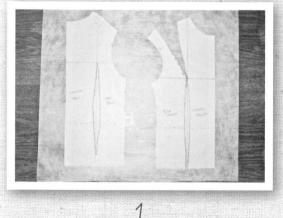

1

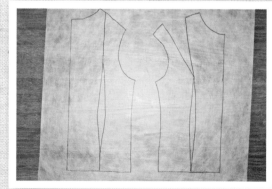

2

1 Lay your body block pieces on the table and cover them with Fabri-Baste. Leave enough room between the pieces to add seam allowances.

2 Trace carefully around each piece, marking in all the darts.

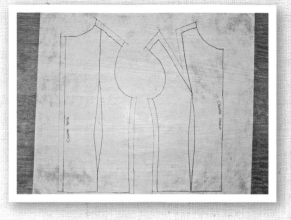

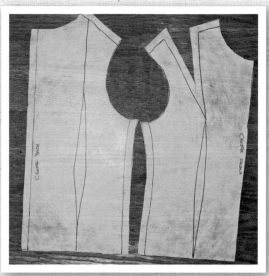

3 Using your designer's square, mark in a ⅝ in (1.5cm) seam allowance on the centre back, side seams and shoulder. Now do the same for the front shoulder dart (**3a**).

Cut out the resulting pattern pieces carefully (**3b**).

4 Next, lay out a pressed piece of calico. Fold it selvedge to selvedge with the fold towards you.

Lay the centre-front pattern piece on the fabric, with the centre-front line on the fold of the fabric. This will ensure that the pattern is lying on the straight grain of the fabric. (I'll tell you more about this later, when we come to make up a real dress.) Pin in place through all the layers.

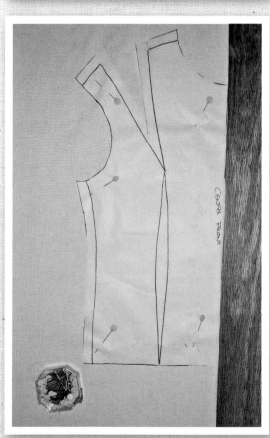

4

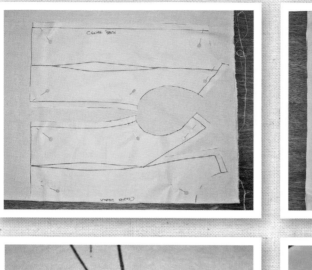

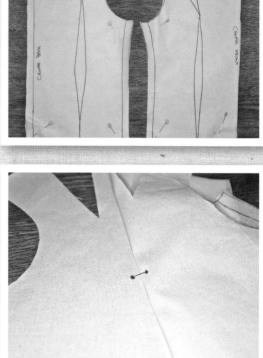

5 Lay the back pattern piece on the fabric alongside the first one. Measure from the folded edge of the fabric to the straight line above the waist dart, then measure from the fold to the line below the dart. Adjust until these two measurements are the same. This pattern piece is now on the straight grain. Pin in place (**5a**).

Cut out the pieces, being as accurate as you can (**5b**).

6 We now need to mark in the darts. Starting with the front, push a pin through the chest point mark on the pattern, going straight down through all the layers (**6a**). Now, open up the layers of fabric by pulling them apart slowly, so you can just see the pin on both layers.

Mark where the pin comes through the fabric on both layers (**6b**).

Note In real life you would use tailor's chalk that can be easily removed. I have used a marker pen so that you can see what I'm doing more clearly.

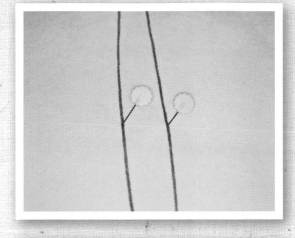

7a

7b

8

9a

9b

7 Close the fabric back up, with the pattern on top, and do the same thing at the widest part of the waist darts to mark them on to the fabric (**7a** and **7b**).

8 Mark the point where the dart runs off the bottom of the pattern with a little snip with your scissors.

9 Now mark the darts on the back in the same way (**9a** and **9b**).

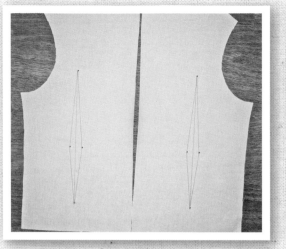

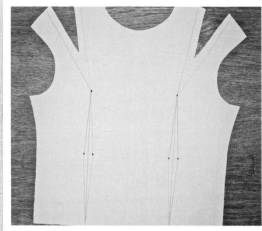

12a

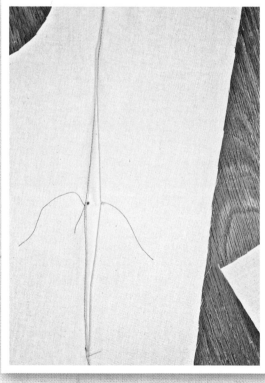

10 With a very fine pencil or tailor's chalk, join up the dart lines to mark the sewing line. Join up the top dart point with the bottom dart point to give you a fold line.

Note You will soon get used to sewing in the darts without the need of these lines, but keep them in until you feel confident with your sewing skills.

12b

11 Now do the same with the front darts. Mark in ⅝ in (1.5cm) seam allowances outside the shoulder-to-chest darts.

12 Sew in the darts, as we did on page 32 (**12a** and **12b**).

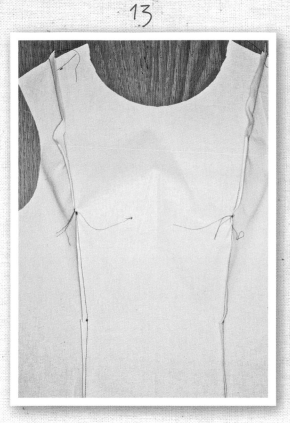

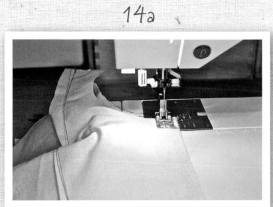

13 Fold the chest darts in half. Stitch using a ⅝in (1.5cm) seam allowance and run off at the chest point.

Don't forget to snip into the darts at the waistline to free up the fabric a little.

14 With the right sides of the fabric together, sew the side seams (**14a** and **14b**). Then sew the shoulder seams (**14c**).

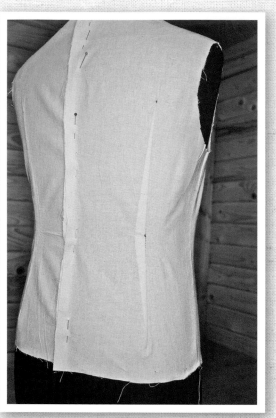

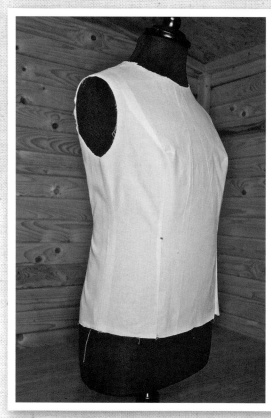

15 Press all darts towards the centre back. Open and press all seams. Try the full block on for size.

Pin in a ⅝in (1.5cm) seam down the back.

16 The block should fit nicely with no obvious pulls or excess fabric. If you have done the job properly then there shouldn't be any alterations needed. However, if it does need adjusting don't panic! Just pin out the excess where needed, mark the adjustments back on your block, re-cut and refit (**16a** and **16b**).

Don't move on to the next part until you have the block just right.

It really is worth doing several blocks. Not only will the fit be perfect, but the sewing part will give you valuable experience, which will make sewing the dresses so much easier!

The Sleeve Block

More of my students have trouble with sleeve blocks than anything else. For some reason they get it into their heads that it's difficult and there's no dissuading them. If you look at a sleeve, it's only a tube with a bit of shape at one end. It isn't hard if you follow the instructions carefully. Go through the process step-by-step, measure accurately and you will be fine.

We are drafting from personal body blocks, so the sleeve measurements will be different for each individual. There are many ways of drafting a sleeve block, but I won't confuse you with them. The technique in this section should work for everyone. It is just a simple, straight, one-piece sleeve, but it is ideal for little girls' dresses. When drafting simple set-in sleeves for my clients, this is exactly the method I use.

A term that will come up frequently in this section is 'ease'. Ease is the amount of extra fabric added depending on how tight or loose you want the finished sleeve. It is always necessary to add some ease, otherwise you won't be able to get the sleeve on. The only exception is if you are using a stretch fabric and want a skin-tight finish. For fitted sleeves, add about 1in (2.5cm) ease to each sleeve width measurement.

We'll start by using this ease measurement for our basic block. You can always add or subtract at the toile stage to produce a different sleeve shape. Using the techniques described below, you will find that the more ease you add to the bicep measurement, the lower the sleeve head will be. It is unlikely that you will use this exact pattern for the dresses. We are going to draft a pattern that fits into the body block, which would be too tight to wear as it is, but we will manipulate this pattern later on to make our final sleeve shapes.

You need to take a few measurements before we start:
- Shoulder point to wrist
- Underarm to wrist
- Around the bicep plus the ease measurement
- Around the wrist plus the ease measurement – make sure that this total measurement is larger than around the fullest part of the hand, otherwise your princess will not be able to get the sleeve on!

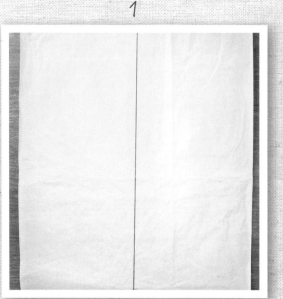

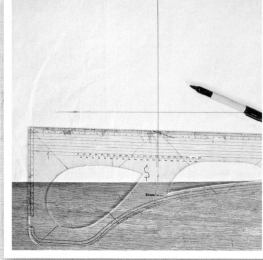

1 We are going to draft the first pattern on paper. Lay out a piece of pattern or brown paper that is longer than the arm by about the same width. Draw a line all the way down the centre of the paper. This will become the centre line of the sleeve. The left-hand side of this line will be the back of the sleeve and the right-hand side will be the front.

2 Next, a little way up from the bottom of the paper, draw a line at right angles to the centre line using your designer's square. We will call this the wrist line.

3 Now measure up from this line with the underarm measurement and mark it on the centre line. Draw a line at right angles to the centre line through this mark. We will call this the bicep line.

3

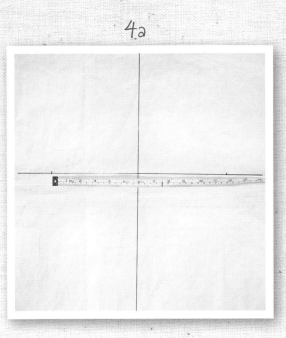

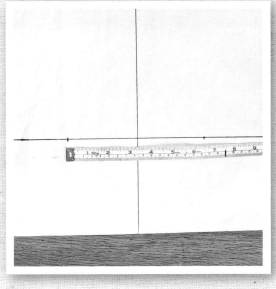

4 Take the bicep measurement plus ease and halve it. Measure this distance either side of the centre line on the bicep line and mark (**4a**).

Do the same with the wrist measurement plus ease on the wrist line (**4b**).

Connect the points (**4c**).

4c

5 Mark the left side of the sleeve as the back and the right side of the sleeve as the front.

6 Take the back body block piece that we made earlier. Place the underarm point on the bicep mark at the back of the sleeve with the curve of the armhole facing in towards the centre line.

Make sure that the shoulder blade line on the block is parallel to the bicep line.

7 Mark in the curve of the armhole to about the blade line on the block.

8 Now do the same thing for the front.

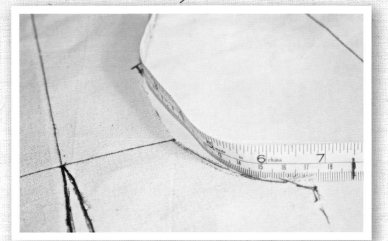

9a

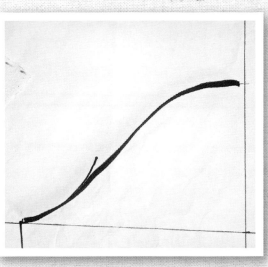

9b

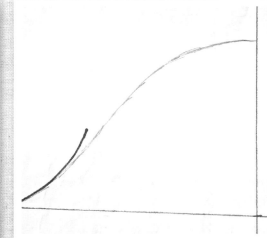

9c

9 With your tape measure on its edge, measure around the back armhole shape from the underarm to the shoulder (**9a**).

Cut a piece of string or non-stretch yarn to this exact measurement. Place one end of the string on the underarm point of the sleeve. Following the line that you drew in from the block, curve the string round and up to the centre line, making the curve as smooth as possible (**9b**).

Draw the line in pencil (**9c**).

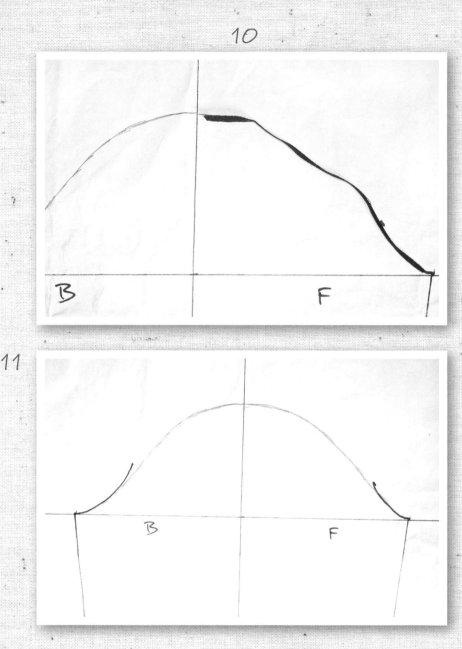

10 Do exactly the same for the front, measuring the front armhole shape in the same way that we did for the back. The curve should meet the back curve at the centre line.

11 Play about with the curve until it runs smoothly with no sharp points. It quite often takes me two or three attempts to get the line running smoothly. You may find the curves on your designer's square are useful for this. Just keep trying until the curves look about right. You can always go back and draft another sleeve block if you are unhappy with the result.

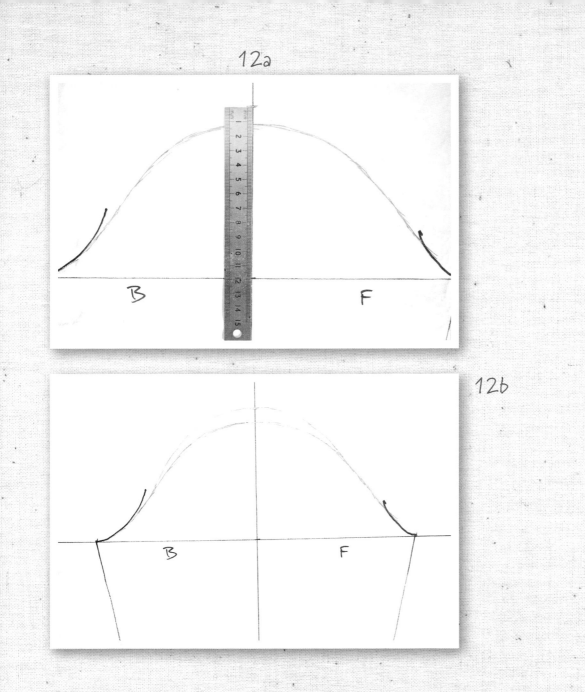

12a

12b

12 Now we need to add some ease to the sleeve head. On the centre line measure up about ½ in (1cm) and make a mark (**12a**).

Now redraw in the sleeve head curve to meet this mark (**12b**).

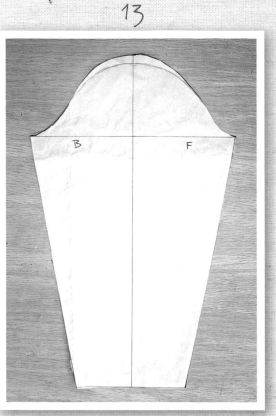

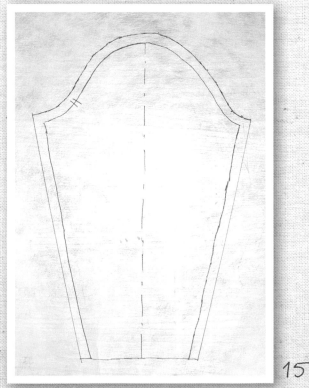

13 Draw over the pencil outline in marker pen. Cut it out and that's your sleeve block finished!

14 Now we need to test the sleeve block to see if it will fit your princess and to make sure it fits into the body block. Draw round the sleeve block on some pattern paper or trace onto a piece of Fabri-Baste.

15 Using your designer's square, add a ⅝in (1.5cm) seam allowance to the sleeve seams and the sleeve head. Add in the centre seam so that you know where the straight grain will be when you cut the sleeve out.

Mark the pattern at the back sleeve head so that you know which is the back when you come to sew.

15

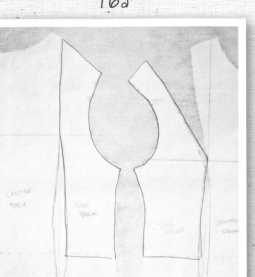

16a

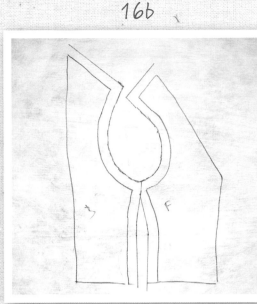

16b

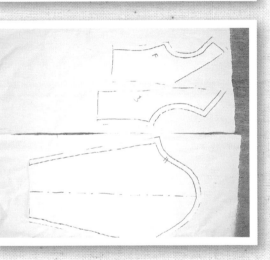

17a

17b

16 Draw round the body block to the dart lines front and back. We don't need to make up a full block, as we only want to test the fit of the sleeve (**16a**).

Add seam allowance to the side, shoulder and armhole seams (**16b**).

17 Cut out one side front, one side back and one sleeve in calico (**17a** and **17b**).

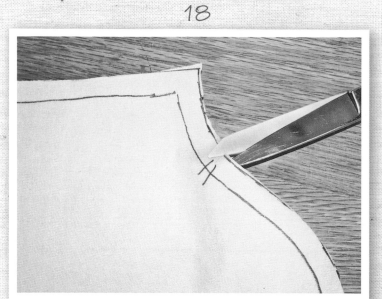

18 Make a little snip into the seam allowance at the back sleeve head so that we know which is the front and which is the back of the sleeve. We call this 'notching'.

19 Sew the side and shoulder seams on to the body.

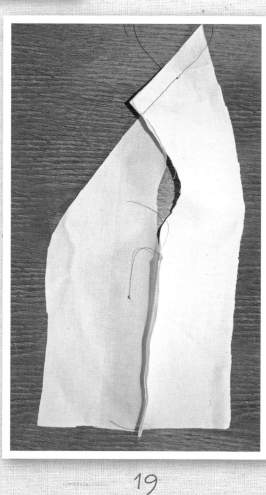

19

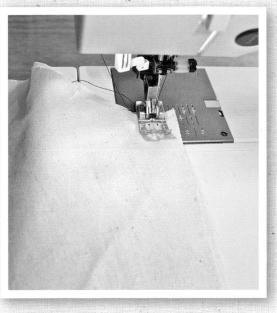

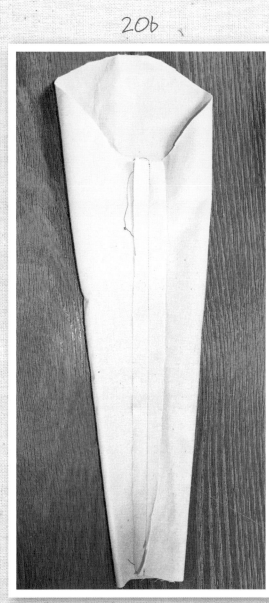

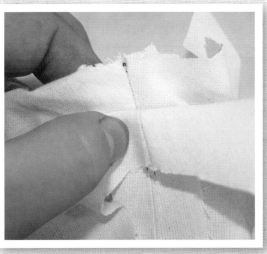

21

20 Sew the sleeve seam (**20a** and **20b**).

21 Make sure that when the sleeve is sewn, the back notch will be at the back of your body block. I frequently make up the sleeve for the wrong side and have to unpick it!

Turn the sleeve through to the right side. With the right sides of the underarm seam and the block side seam facing, pin the sleeve head into the armhole, matching up the seams.

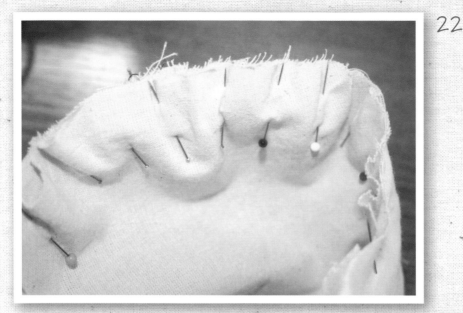

22

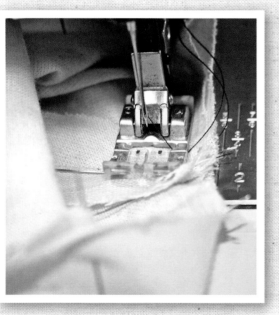

23a

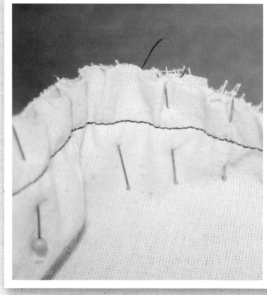

23b

22 You will have to ease the sleeve head in a bit to make it fit, but don't put any pleats in. If you can't get all the sleeve head in then you will have put in too much ease. Go back and redo that part with less ease.

23 Stitch from the inside with the bodice fabric on the bottom and the sleeve fabric on the top (**23a** and **23b**).

You have now been introduced to all the sewing and pattern-cutting techniques needed to make the little best dress of your choice.

At this stage, if there was any principle or technique that you struggled with, go back and do it again. Don't move on to making any dresses until you feel completely confident.

When testing the teaching methods used in this book on friends, most of them couldn't wait to rush ahead and make something. They each reported that they moved on too quickly and had to do some of the sewing techniques again. I want you to be able to cut and make a dress with confidence, without wasting expensive fabrics.

Students who don't believe they can follow sewing projects from books are normally the ones who move on to the next section too soon. Consequently, they lose confidence and put the book away. I want you to leave this book out the whole time, work slowly and thoroughly and enjoy the rewards when you make your princess her very own designer gown!

24

24 The sleeve should fit snugly and without any obvious pulls or wrinkles. Make any adjustments necessary and refit the sleeve if you need to.

The Dresses

'Her fairy godmother then touched her with her wand, and, at the same instant, her clothes turned into cloth of gold and silver, all beset with jewels.'

CINDERELLA

Basic Shapes

Now that you have made the body and sleeve blocks, you need to know how to manipulate them into different dress styles. You can then put together the bodice, sleeve and skirt designs in any way you choose, in any length and in any fabric.

Study the dresses shown over the following pages; look closely at how they have been cut and constructed. I would strongly suggest that, at this stage, you make one or two of these designs so that you can understand the processes that are used.

By putting these bodice, sleeve and skirt styles together in different combinations and different lengths, there are potentially hundreds of design options. Add the different neckline shapes and you can create many more.

Let's look at the design possibilities for each individual element of your own little best dress.

Skirt styles

A-line This can be cut in one piece, in two pieces (a front and a back), or as panels.

Straight Longer length skirts will need a split up the back or side seam to the knee so that your princess can walk!

Full circle This is ideal when you want a full-skirted design without the bulk made by gathering at the waist.

Gathered Probably the simplest but most effective style of skirt.

Bodice shapes

Full This is the bodice shape we will use if we are going to add sleeves.

Sleeveless This is the one we will use if we are not adding sleeves.

Empire line All of the bodice shapes can be cut to just under the bust to make them empire line.

Strappy You can make the straps out of your main fabric, ribbon or lingerie elastic. The straps may be either tied at the shoulder or set into the top bodice seam.

Halterneck You can cut this to tie at the back neck or make the halterneck shape at the back and fasten with a zip or buttons.

Sleeve shapes

Straight You already have the straight sleeve shape, which is the basic sleeve block we made. This can be cut to any length.

Gathered Enlarge the sleeve head and gather it in to the shoulder seam. Again, this can be cut at any length.

Puff This sleeve shape is gathered at the sleeve head and into a cuff.

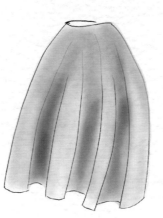

A-line skirt   Straight skirt   Full circle skirt   Gathered skirt

Full bodice   Sleeveless bodice   Empire line bodice

Strappy bodice   Halterneck bodice

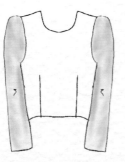
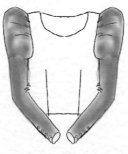

Straight sleeve   Gathered sleeve   Puff sleeve

Choosing Your Fabrics

The choice of fabric in stores, markets and on-line nowadays is dazzling, and can be confusing, so take your time – even a dress that is designed and made well can easily be spoiled if you choose the wrong fabric.

The fabric that you choose for your design is dictated by several factors. Ask yourself these questions when deciding on the perfect fabric:

- How often will it be worn?
- Will I need to machine-wash it or is it okay for it to be dry-clean only?
- Does it need to be stiff and structured or soft and floaty?
- Is the colour right for her skin tone?
- How many colours do I need for my design and should they all be in the same fabric?
- Is the fabric strong enough to support any trims or embellishments that I may want to use?
- Can I afford it and, if not, is there a cheaper alternative?

When you have answered all of these questions, you should be on the way to finding the perfect fabric for your design.

Fabric manufacturers are bringing out new designs and fabric types all the time. Take advice from your local fabric store; show the staff your design and ask them which fabric they recommend for the project. Trust them – fabric stores want your return custom. It is unlikely that they will sell you the wrong fabric type as they want to see

SHOT SILK TAFFETA: ❶
SILK TAFFETA: ❷
SILK DUPION: ❸ ❹ ❺
PRINTED COTTON: ❻
CRUSHED CRYSTAL ORGANZA: ❼
VELVET: ❽
CORDED LACE: ❾

2 **3** **4** **5** **6** **7** **8**

you again! Here are a few of my favourite fabrics for children's wear designs, but it is by no means a definitive list:

Silk dupion

Dupion, or dupioni, is probably the fabric that I use most for structured occasion wear, both for adults and children. Pure silk has a real sense of luxury and occasion. There is something about the feel of silk next to the skin that no other fabric can achieve. There is even something about the noise it makes when you move in it that makes you feel special. Imagine the gentle 'shush' that the gown will make as your princess makes her entrance – fashionably late, of course.

Dupion comes in a massive range of colours and is available in hand weaves and machine weaves. I tend to go for the machine weave, sometimes called Chinese dupion, because it is more tightly woven and therefore more hard-wearing than its Indian, hand-woven, counterpart.

The fabric is usually 'piece-dyed', which means it is dyed after it is woven, so it can sometimes change shade ever so slightly along the length of the roll. With this in mind, always buy enough fabric to finish your project because, even if you go back and buy more fabric off the same roll, it can be quite a different colour when you get it home.

Taffeta

Taffeta is available in both natural and man-made varieties. To be honest, with modern manufacturing techniques, there isn't a great deal of difference between the two except, of course, the price. Taffeta is much stiffer than dupion and is mostly used for more structured designs. The tighter weave of the fabric often shows pin marks, especially with the man-made varieties, so be careful to pin only within the seam allowance. Also be careful when you press taffeta: seam lines can show through as a shiny line on the right side of the garment if you are too heavy-handed with your iron.

Organza

Organza, or organdie, is a sheer fabric that comes in silk and man-made varieties. It is a lightweight fabric with some body and stiffness, making it ideal to use as overlays on full skirts, or when you want to have a transparent sleeve for a lighter look. There are many types, from the plain, matt finish of plain organza to the spectacular shine and sparkle of crystal organza. Again, your fabric supplier will help you choose.

Organza can be quite difficult to sew and tends to pucker up a little when sewn with long seams. Loosen your tension a little, use a very sharp, fine, new needle and sew with a shorter stitch length to make things a little easier. If your machine is dragging the fabric into the needle hole, try sewing with a little tissue paper or embroidery stabilizer in the seams, and carefully rip it out when the seam is complete.

Printed cotton

Cotton is a very hard-wearing fabric that is easy to sew and care for. You can wash it at fairly high temperatures, making it the ideal choice for the little princess who likes to throw more ice cream down herself than she eats!

There are thousands of fabulous prints out there if you look for them. Don't restrict yourself to dressmaking fabrics; you may find the perfect print in the quilting section or even in the home furnishing section of your fabric store. Make sure that you check out the furnishings and drapes of the party venue – you don't want your princess to disappear when she sits down!

Lace

There are many different types of lace and you really do get exactly what you pay for. Buy small pieces of lace and experiment to get the look you want. Choose the most expensive lace you can afford, as cheap lace looks just that: cheap.

Some lace is actually embroidery on fine net. This looks good used as an overlay, when the main fabric and the lace are sewn together as though one fabric. All-over corded lace has a border on each side, which can be cut away and used to edge hems and necklines. Guipure lace is expensive, but can look beautiful used sparingly as single motifs, either alone or mixed with all-over corded lace.

Chiffon

Again this can be either silk or man-made. It is a much lighter, floatier fabric than organza, making it suitable for draping. It also looks really good in layered designs. Try using three or four layers, with each layer a slightly lighter colour than the one beneath for spectacular results.

Velvet

Velvet is lovely, but it's a notoriously difficult fabric to work with. It has a 'nap', or pile, which all lies in one direction. If you make a mistake and stitch a seam with the nap up on one side and down on the other, the velvet will reflect light differently, and the panels will look to be completely different colours.

Because of its pile, velvet is quite hard to stitch and to press. It is very easy to mark the fabric, either with the iron or even with the presser foot on your machine. Pressing is easier if you use a commercially available velvet board or you can just use a piece of scrap velvet with the pile up on your ironing board (which is easier and cheaper).

Velvet comes in silk, cotton or man-made versions. Man-made velvet is usually rayon or a rayon and silk mix. On the latter, the pile can be burnt out using chemicals to produce a very beautiful devore velvet.

Rose

'Queen rose of the rosebud garden of girls...
In gloss of satin and glimmer of pearls...
Shine out, little head, sunning over with curls'

COME INTO THE GARDEN MAUD
Alfred Lord Tennyson

Rose

This is the prettiest little flower fairy dress.
It looks quite complicated but, even though there
are a lot of stages, it's really very easy.

You will learn some valuable techniques by making this dress. Even if you don't make the dress as it is, I would strongly suggest you give the bodice a go, as we will be using the same techniques for all the other dresses. The first thing we need to do is make the bodice pattern. This is a very important lesson, as we are going to manipulate the body block into a dress pattern for the first time. So, let's start – exciting isn't it?

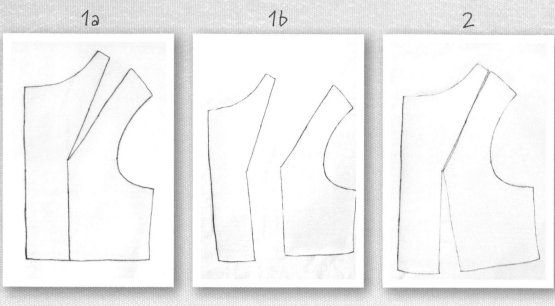

Making the pattern

1 Take your body block – this is the one that's only half a body, without the seam allowances added. Trace over the block on to Fabri-Baste. We are making a bodice to the waist, so that's the only part we need to trace. Trace all construction lines. Mine is for a four-year-old so there was no front waist dart. If there is one on yours, trace it in. If not, just draw in the straight line (**1a**). Then cut out along the lines (**1b**).

2 Now, remember the shoulder-to-bust dart that we started with? We are going to 'throw' this dart into the waist dart. Join up the bust dart at the top with sticky tape, and see how the dart has moved to the waist!

3 Do exactly the same thing for the back. Trace the back block including all the darts.

4 Join up the shoulder dart, thereby throwing the shoulder dart into the waist. Now we are going to design the shape of the bodice. Lay the front and back pattern pieces together at the side seams. Draw

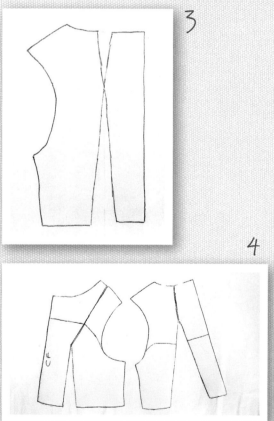

in a top bodice line on the front and back pieces with a smooth curve. This can be any way you like depending on your design.

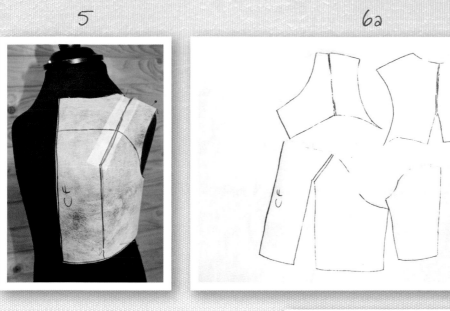

5

6a

5 Cut out and pin the Fabri-Baste in place on your princess to make sure that the top line is in the right place. Adjust the line if necessary. Remember that we haven't included any seam allowances yet.

6 Now we are going to eliminate some of the seams to make the bodice easier to sew later. Lay the front and the back patterns together at the side seams. Cut out along the top lines (**6a**).

6b

Join up the side seams and the back dart seam with sticky tape (**6b**).

7 Trace all around this new shape. Add a ⅜in (1.5cm) seam allowance to the centre-back seam for the zip and the same for the waistline. Add a ½in (1cm) seam allowance to the top line and to the front dart. And that's your bodice pattern done! How simple was that?

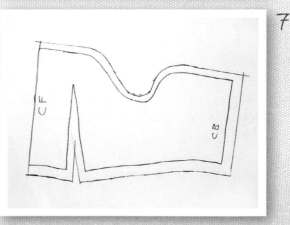

7

8a

8b

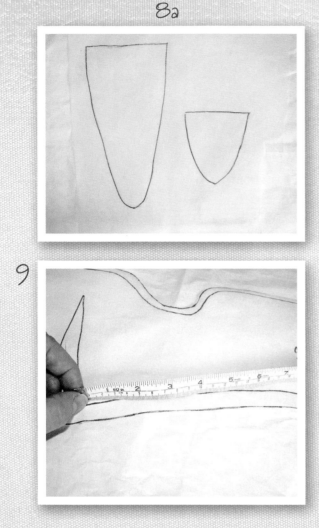

9

Little Tip

I've done long, fuchsia-style petals, but you can make the petals any shape that you like. Look at your favourite flower for inspiration.

8 Now for the petal pattern. On a piece of pattern paper, draw a rectangle of the length that you want the petals to be, with a width of about a third of the length. Fold the paper in half lengthways. Draw on the half petal shape, curving the 'sharp end' slightly. Do the same for the shoulder petals. Trace the petal shapes on to some Fabri-Baste or tracing paper (**8a**).

Add a ⅜in (1.5cm) seam allowance to the waist edge and a ¼in (0.5cm) seam allowance to the petal edges (**8b**). Cut out the petal patterns.

9 Now we're ready for the next stage of pattern making: the full circle skirt layers. The first thing that we need to know is the waist circumference. With your tape measure on its edge, measure on the sewing line (not the added seam allowance line) from the centre front to the dart stitching line. Now measure from the next dart stitching line to the centre-back line. Add these two measurements together and double it. This is the bodice waist circumference.

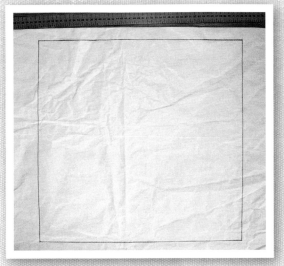

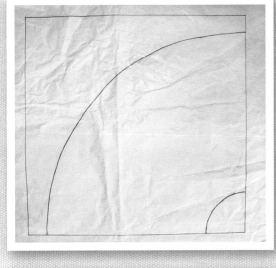

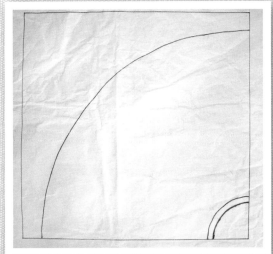

Divide this measurement by 3.142, then divide this number by 2. This is the radius of the inner circle. Decide how long you want the skirt to be. Add this measurement to the inner radius measurement. This is the radius of the outer circle.

10 On a piece of paper draw a square that's about 2in (5cm) bigger each way than the outer radius measurement.

11 Take your tape measure or a piece of string cut to the exact measurement of the inner radius. Centre it in one corner of the square and strike an ark to give you quarter of a circle. Now do the same thing for the outer radius.

12 Add a ⅝in (1.5cm) seam allowance to the waist seam (inner radius), the side nearest the corner. We don't need to add a seam allowance to the hem as we are going to overcast it.

This is exactly the technique that you will use whenever you want to draft a full circle skirt pattern.

And that's the pattern done!

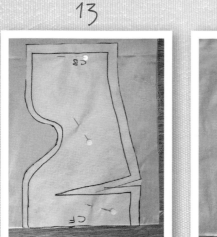

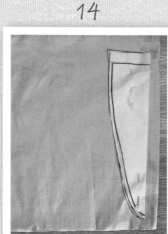

16

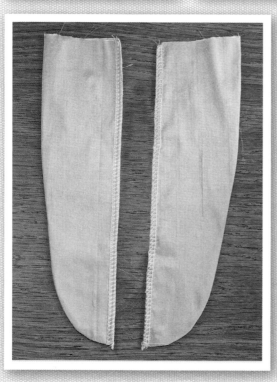

14 We are going to split one of the petals down the middle for the zip. Fold two pieces of fabric selvedge to selvedge and lay the folds on top of each other, giving four layers of fabric. Fold the main petal pattern in half lengthways and lay it ⅝in (1.5cm) away from the folds of the fabric – this will form the seam allowance for the zip. Cut out around the pattern. Then cut down both the folds.

15 Open up the petal pattern and lay it on the same folded fabric with the top of the pattern running parallel to the selvedge. This will make the petal sit on the straight grain. Cut out (this will create four petal pieces, which will be two petals once sewn and turned through). Repeat until you have enough petals for your desired look. I used eight petals plus the two half petals.

The dress

13 Fold your fabric selvedge to selvedge. This will make the fold on the straight grain of the fabric. Pin the bodice pattern on the fabric with the 'cf' mark on the fold of the fabric. Then cut it out. The bodice takes such a small amount of fabric, I've cut the lining out of the main fabric as well.

16 Take two half petal pieces and lay them on top of each other, right sides together. Stitch down the long curved side using a ¼in (0.5cm) seam allowance.

Turn through to the right side. Press, making sure that the curve runs smoothly. Repeat for the other half petal. Overlock or overcast down the long straight edges.

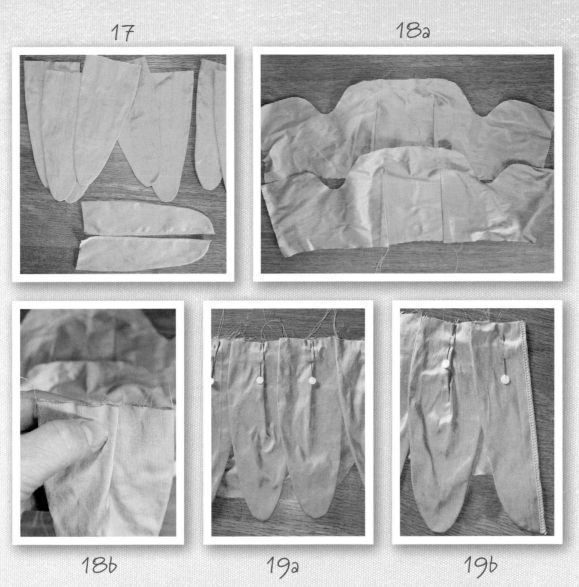

17 Make up your remaining full petals. Use the same seam allowance and stitch round the whole petal, leaving the top straight edge open. Turn through and press.

18 With petals done, now we can do the bodice and bodice lining. Mark in and stitch the front darts, exactly as we did for the full block, on both the bodice and the lining pieces (**18a**).

Take one of your petals and fold in a little pleat at the top open edge (**18b**).

19 With right sides together, pin the petal to the main bodice piece. Pin it to the centre of the waist edge, with the point of the petal pointing towards the shoulder.

Repeat for the remaining petals, spacing them evenly around the waist edge. Overlap the petals as required – it will depend on how many you are using (**19a**).

Finish with a half petal on either side, lining the straight edge up with the centre-back edge (**19b**).

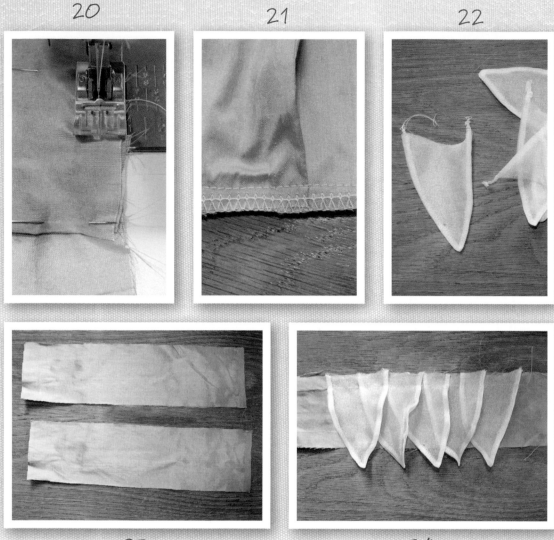

20 Sew the seam using a ⅝in (1.5cm) seam allowance.

21 Overlock or overcast the raw seam to neaten it.

22 Now for the shoulder straps. Cut out and sew the shoulder petals just as we did for the main petals. I used 12 and made them in organza.

23 Measure the required length for your shoulder straps and add about 3in (7.5cm). Cut out two strips of main fabric of this length by 3¼in (8.25cm).

24 Take one length of fabric and half the shoulder petals. Pin the petals down one long edge, leaving about 1in (2.5cm) free at each end.

Stitch a ⅝in (1.5cm) seam.

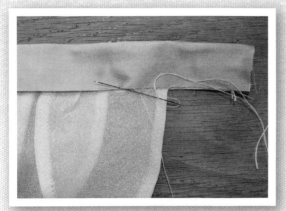

25

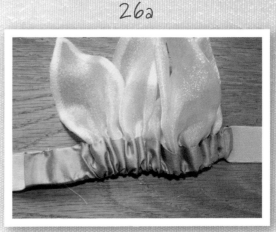

26a

26b

27

28

25 Fold in the seam allowance and press. Fold in the same amount of seam allowance on the other long edge and press. Fold in half lengthways and hand-stitch closed.

26 Cut a piece of 1in (2.5cm) elastic – when slightly stretched it should be the same length as the straps. Thread it through your strap (**26a**).

Stitch the ends of the strap securely to the ends of the elastic (**26b**).

27 Take your bodice lining and overlock or overcast the centre-back seams and the waist seam.

28 With right sides together, pin the shoulder straps to the front main bodice, level with the bust darts.

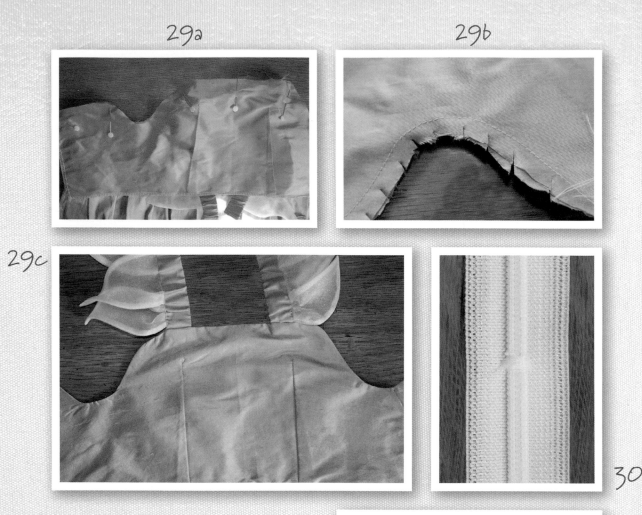

29a

29b

29c

30

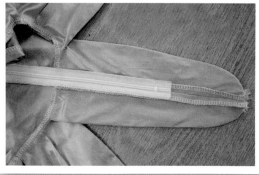

31

29 With right sides together, pin the bodice lining to the main bodice along the top seam, trapping the shoulder straps in between (**29a**).

Being careful not to catch the petals, stitch a ½ in (1cm) seam across the entire top of the bodice. Snip into the curves (**29b**). Turn through and press (**29c**). Hey, it's starting to look like a dress!

30 Now for the zip. Measure down the back seam to about halfway down the petal. Measure the same length on the zip, from the top, and mark. Zigzag over the teeth of the zip to secure. Cut off the excess.

31 Now insert the zip exactly as we did in the basic sewing section (see pages 40–43). Finish off sewing the petal seam and press.

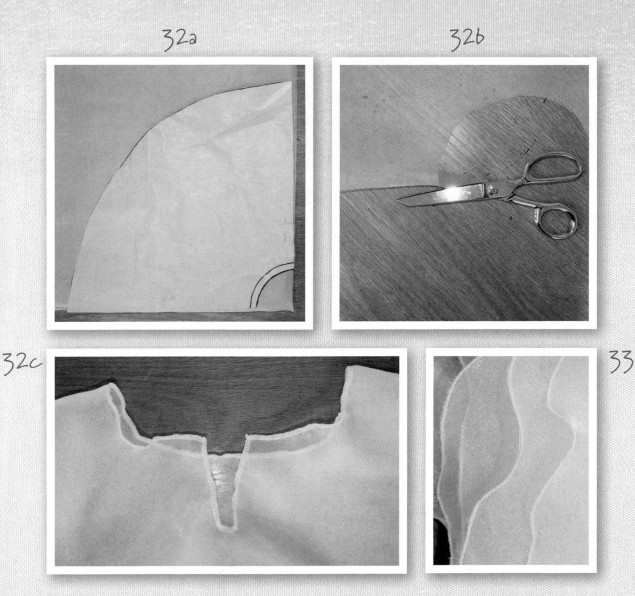

32a

32b

32c

33

32 We haven't got far to go now. Fold a square of organza fabric into quarters, with the folds towards you and to the right. Lay the quarter circle pattern on the fabric as shown (**32a**).

Cut and open out to half a circle. Cut down one fold, from the centre circle, about 3in (7.5cm) (**32b**).

Overlock or overcast all round the centre circle and the split (**32c**).

33 Finish off the hem of the organza by running a very small zigzag stitch around it. Position your fabric under the machine foot so that when the needle swings to the left, it goes into the fabric, but when it swings to the right it goes just off the edge. This will make a very neat edge. It might help to practise on a scrap of fabric if you are unsure.

34

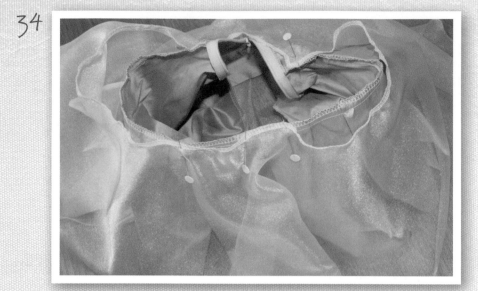

35

36

34 Pin the organza skirt to the main bodice with the split opening at the zip seam. Effectively, you are sandwiching the petals between the bodice and the organza. Sew the seam following the stitching line at the waist on the bodice.

35 Make up a four-layer underskirt, of the right length for your dress, just as we did in the net underskirt section (see pages 48–51).

36 Sew the underskirt on to the waist seam, as we did before. Use zigzag stitch to keep the seam flat.

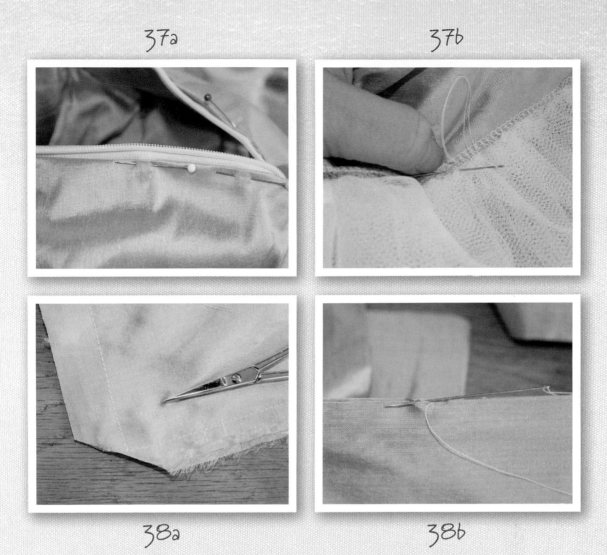

37a

37b

38a

38b

37 Fold in the lining at the centre back, pin and hand-stitch in place (**37a**). Then hand-stitch the lining down, over the net, at the waist seam (**37b**).

38 The last element of the design is the sash. This is very simple. Just cut a length of fabric to the desired length by twice the width, plus twice the seam allowance. Fold in half lengthways and stitch across the ends and down the long open side. Leave about 3in (7.5cm) unstitched somewhere along the seam to allow you to turn the sash through. Clip off the corners (**38a**).

Turn through to the right side. I use a large knitting needle to push the corners out. Press and hand-stitch the opening closed (**38b**).

And that's your first little best dress done!

Now, I'll let you into a secret: this was probably the most difficult dress in the book! Now that you've done this one, you will find the rest of them a piece of cake.

Bluebells

'O, that lone flower recalled to me
My happy childhood's hours
When bluebells seemed like fairy gifts
A prize among the flowers'

THE BLUEBELL
Anne Brontë

Bluebells

Being a bridesmaid or flower girl is probably the first chance
that your princess will get to wear a beautiful gown in public.
Spoil her. Use the best fabrics that you can afford. Spend time
adding some couture finishes, like the satin ribbon hem on
the underskirt or a hand-bound hem on the dress.

In the following pages, I will show you three bridesmaids' dresses for girls aged 4, 8 and 12 – although you can make them for any age you wish. Each dress pattern will teach you something new.

I've used the most exquisite Italian silk taffeta in ivory, with contrast trims of bluebell silk dupion. What I love most about taffeta is the noise it makes! Listen for the gentle 'whoosh' as your princess makes her grand entrance.

Bluebell 1

This dress has a full circle skirt and little puff sleeves – it's perfect for younger bridesmaids!

1

1 Trace out the body block and throw the darts into the waist seam, just as we did for *Rose* (see page 104).

2 Now drop the front neckline by ⅝in (1.5cm) (**2a**).

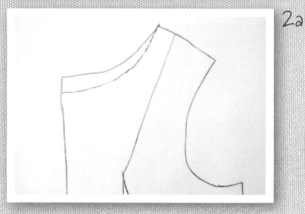
2a

Add a ⅝in (1.5cm) seam allowance to the shoulders, armholes, centre-back seam and the waist edges (**2b**).

We are going to ignore the waist darts for this design, as the sash is going to pull the bodice in at the waist. And, as we are going to bind the neck edge, there is no need to add seam allowance here.

From now on we will assume that all seam allowances are ⅝in (1.5cm), unless it is otherwise stated.

2b

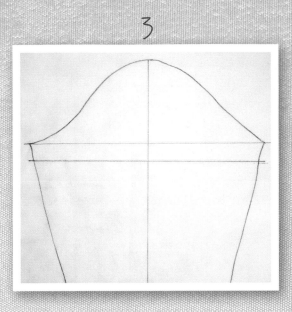

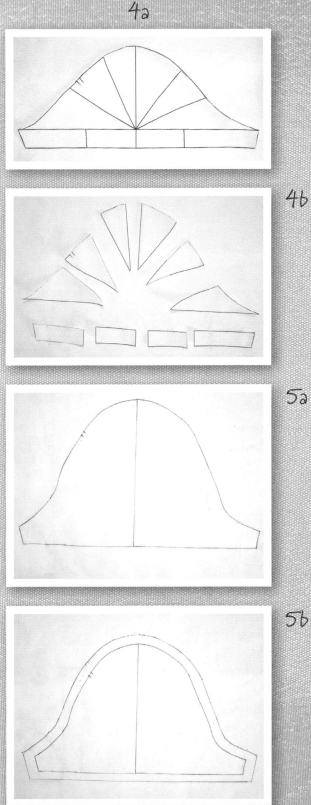

3 Draft a sleeve block for the bodice – see page 79. Draw in a line to mark the sleeve length. As I want my sleeve to be very short, I've drawn mine in just under the bicep line.

4 Cut out the new sleeve shape along the lines. Now we are going to draw in 'explode' lines. Divide the sleeve into ten sections, as shown (**4a**).

Cut out along these lines, being careful to leave the pieces in order. You may want to label the pieces, if this helps. Move them outwards as shown (**4b**). This is called 'exploding the shape'. The bigger the new shape, the puffier the sleeve.

5 Draw round the exploded pattern pieces and make a mark to remind you which is the back arm (**5a**).

Add seam allowance (**5b**) and cut out.

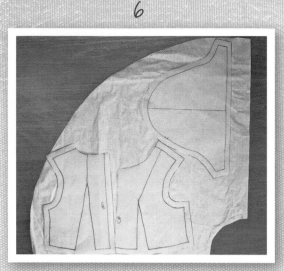

6 Make a circular skirt pattern using the new waist measurement plus 1¼ in (3cm). It is the same process as on pages 106–7, but without the darts.

And that's all the pattern pieces done! How easy was that?

7 Cut out the skirt in your main fabric, just as we did for *Rose*. Open out the skirt so that it is a semi-circle. Cut down one fold, from the waist to the hem, to make the back seam.

8 Cut out another circle skirt in lining fabric, making the length slightly shorter than the main fabric skirt. Then cut another skirt in net, making this one slightly shorter than the lining. Cut the back seam for both skirts, but only cut about 6in (15cm) down from the waist.

9 Overlock or overcast the hems, waist and back seams of the main fabric and the lining. Zigzag a length of satin ribbon round the hem of the net (see Net Underskirts, page 46).

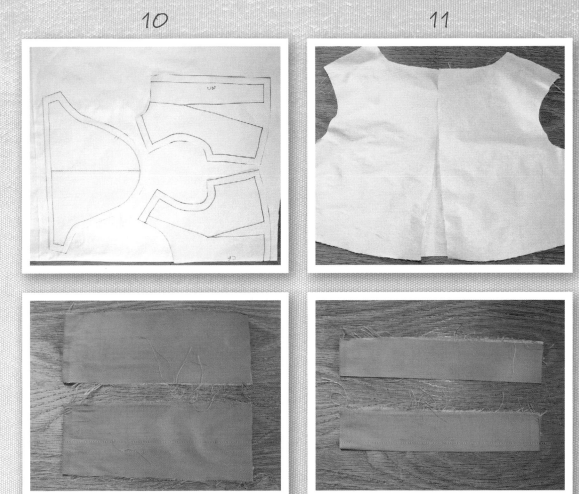

10

11

12a

12b

10 Lay out the bodice and sleeve pieces on your fabric, making sure that the centre front is on the fold of the fabric. Cut out. The bodice only uses a small amount of fabric, so I also used the same fabric to make the bodice lining.

11 Place the front and back bodice pieces right sides together. Stitch the side and shoulder seams.

12 Now we will make up the sleeves. Measure the bicep, or upper arm, of your princess. Cut two pieces of fabric for the sleeve trim: length should be the bicep measurement, plus a little for ease, plus twice the seam allowance; the width should be twice the width of the finished trim plus twice the seam allowance (**12a**).

Press the pieces in half lengthways (**12b**).

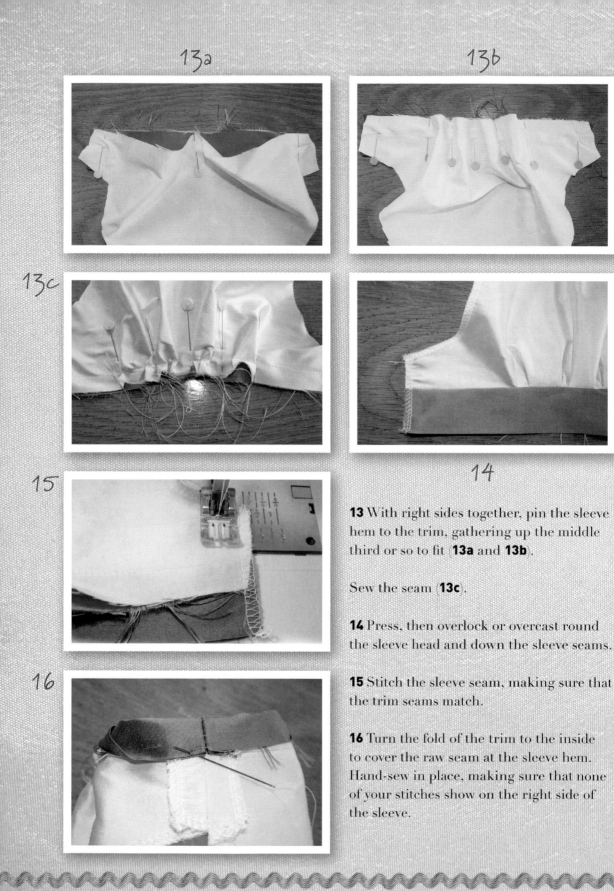

13a

13b

13c

14

15

16

13 With right sides together, pin the sleeve hem to the trim, gathering up the middle third or so to fit (**13a** and **13b**).

Sew the seam (**13c**).

14 Press, then overlock or overcast round the sleeve head and down the sleeve seams.

15 Stitch the sleeve seam, making sure that the trim seams match.

16 Turn the fold of the trim to the inside to cover the raw seam at the sleeve hem. Hand-sew in place, making sure that none of your stitches show on the right side of the sleeve.

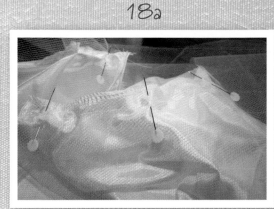

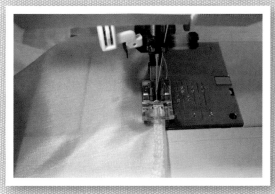

19a

19b

17 Now for the lining. Sew the side and shoulder seams just as we did for the main bodice. Press in the centre-back seams just over ⅝in (1.5cm).

18 With right sides together, pin the skirt lining and the net to the waist seam of your bodice (**18a**).

If your calculations and cutting were accurate, these should fit exactly. But don't worry too much if you have to pin a little tuck here and there, as the sash will cover a multitude of sins! Sew the seam (**18b**).

19 Turn up the lining hem by the width of the overlocked edge and stitch (**19a**).

And that's the lining done (**19b**).

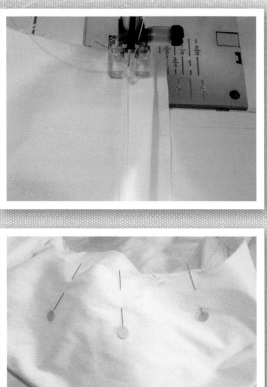

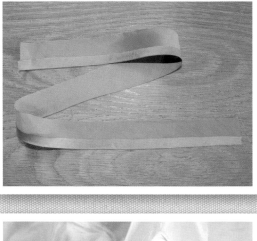

22

23a

20 Sew the main skirt to the bodice just as we did for the lining.

Sew in a concealed zip (see page 40) to finish, about 6in (15cm) down the skirt.

Sew the back skirt seam and finish the hem as we did for the lining. However, you could do a bias-bagged hem if you feel like sitting for hours to hand-sew it in place!

21 Cut a piece of contrast bias strip that is 1½in (4cm) wide. The length needs to be one and a half times the circumference of the neck edge. Press in one long side by ½in (1cm).

22 With the wrong sides together, pin the lining inside the main bodice at the neck edge.

23 With the unfolded edge of the bias binding at the neck edge and the folded edge folding towards you (as shown), fold a little of the binding around the zip edge and pin (**23a**).

Using a ½in (1cm) seam allowance, sew the binding into place at the neck edge, being careful not to stretch it (**23b**).

When you get to the other zip seam, trim off the binding so that you can fold a little of it round the zip, as shown (**23c**).

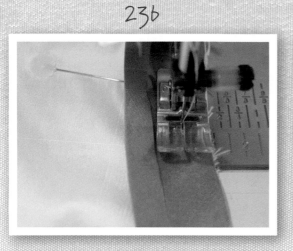

23b

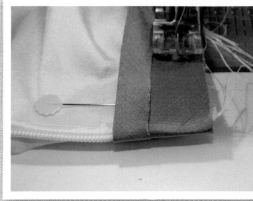

23c

24a

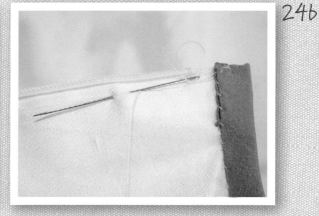

24b

25

24 Open up the binding and hand-stitch into place on the inside (**24a**).

Hand-sew the lining to the zip tape along the folded edge (**24b**).

25 Overlock or overcast the main fabric and lining armholes together, being careful to match the shoulder seams and the underarm seams.

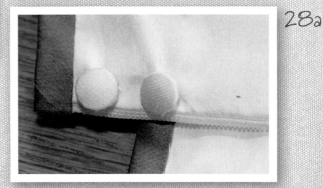

26 Pin and set in the sleeve, gathering the sleeve head to fit (**26a** and **26b**).

Turn through to the right side (**26c**).

27 Make a sash just like we did for *Rose* (see page 115) and try the dress on your princess. Place a pin on the back seam to mark where the top of the sash should be.

28 Mark and sew on some covered buttons, spacing them evenly between the neck edge and the pin mark (**28a** and **28b**).

And that's the dress finished!

Bluebell 2

This dress may look complicated but it is actually quite easy to construct. The only slight difficulty is in the amount of fabric that you will have to handle when making the gathers at the waist. Take your time and you'll do just fine.

1 Trace the body block to the waist and throw the darts into the waist, just as we've done before.

2 As we're not putting sleeves in this design, narrow the shoulders slightly at the shoulder edge. Now square off the neckline to the desired shape (**2a**).

Add a ⅝in (1.5cm) seam allowance to the side seams, shoulder seams, waistline and centre back. Add a ½in (1cm) seam allowance to the front and back neckline and armholes (**2b**).

Now, believe it or not, that's the pattern finished!

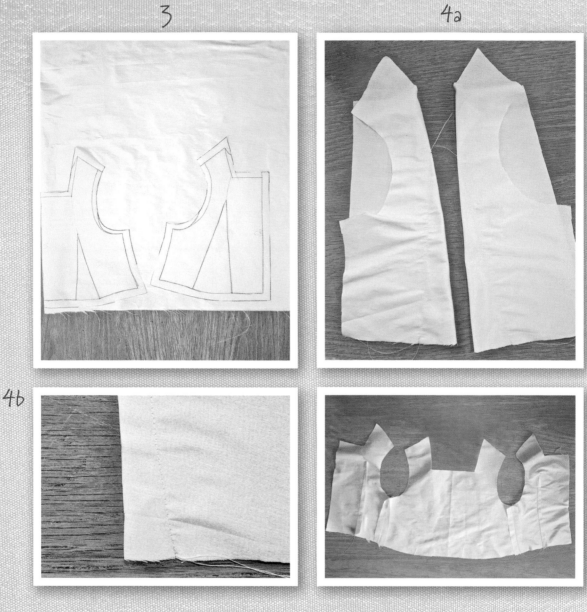

3 Place the centre front of the bodice pattern on the fold of the fabric. Place the back bodice pattern next to it, making sure that the centre-back line runs parallel to the fabric fold. This will ensure that the fabric is on 'the straight grain'. The bodice uses such a small amount of fabric that I have cut the lining from the same fabric; however, you could use a coordinating lining if you wish.

4 Mark in and stitch the back darts only. We are going to ignore the front darts to give us a little ease in the waist (**4a**).

Trim down the excess fabric in the dart to about ½ in (1cm) (**4b**).

5 With right sides together, sew the side seams and press them open. Press the dart seams towards the centre back. Repeat for the lining.

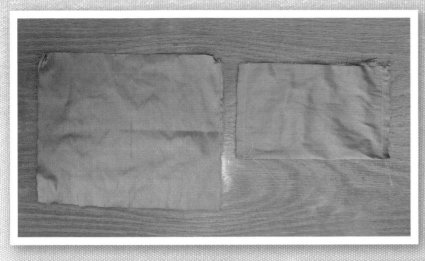

7

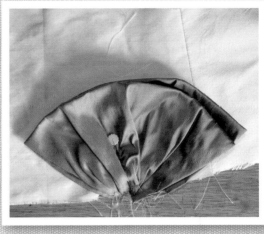

8

6 Now we're going to make the rosette bow that sets into the waist seam. First decide how big you want the bow to be. Cut two squares of fabric that are twice the required length, plus ¾in (2cm) by the required width, plus ¾in (2cm). Fold in half top to bottom and sew the side seams with a ½in (1cm) seam allowance.

Note I can't give you exact measurements here, as the size of your bow should relate proportionately to the size of your dress. Just do what you think is the right size. You can always adjust as you go.

7 Turn through to the right side. Gather up the open end to form half of your rosette and sew. Repeat for the bottom half.

8 Pin one bow on top of the other, to the right side of the fabric at the waistline; position it where you like. I think the best place is between where the bust dart would have been and the side seam.

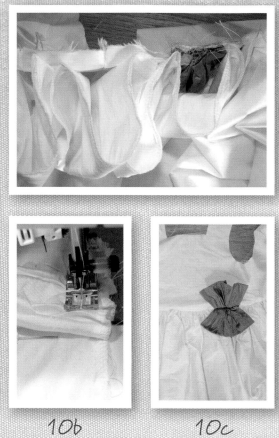

9 Now let's cut the skirt. Decide how wide you want your bottom contrast band to be. Cut three lengths of the contrast fabric: this should be twice the desired width of the contrast band, plus two seam allowances, by the width of the fabric. Sew the short edges together to make one long strip. Overlock the raw edges.

Cut three lengths of the main skirt fabric. This should be the length of the skirt minus the width of the finished contrast band, plus two seam allowances. Sew them together down the short sides to make one long strip and overlock top and bottom.

Now place the contrast panel and main skirt right sides together. Stitch one overlocked long seam of the contrast panel to one long seam of the main skirt. Press the seam open.

10 Now for the gathers. You may think to yourself, 'How on earth will I get all that fabric gathered into that little waist seam?' Well, just take your time. Use the third method in the gathering section (see page 28) and with right sides of the fabric together, gather and sew the skirt on to the bodice (**10a**).

Leave about 1in (2.5cm) of fabric ungathered at the centre-back seams, where we are going to insert the zip and make slightly less gathering over the rosette bow (**10b** and **10c**).

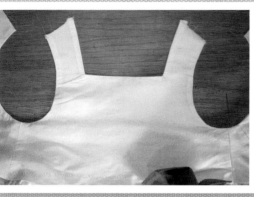

14a

14b

11 Overlock or overcast the waist seam of the bodice lining. Then, with right sides together, pin the bodice lining to the main bodice at the back neck, armholes and front neck.

12 Next, sew a ½in (1cm) seam around the armholes and necklines (don't go across the shoulder seams at this point). Snip into the armhole curves and into the corners of the front and back neckline.

13 Turn through to the right side and press, making sure that you can't see any lining from the front.

14 Now for the shoulder seams. Tuck the front shoulder seams to the inside by about 1in (2.5cm) (**14a**).

Push the back shoulder into it (**14b**).

16a

15 Reach inside, up between the lining and the main fabric, and pull through, holding on to the shoulders as you do so (**15a**).

Line up the seams and stitch (**15b**).

Snip across the corners, to get rid of some bulk, and pull through. Press and you have the perfect shoulder seam (**15c**).

16 Insert a concealed zip, as before and sew down the back skirt seam (**16a**).

Sew the lining to the zip tape (**16b**).

16b

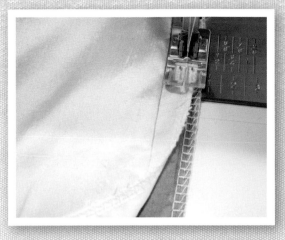

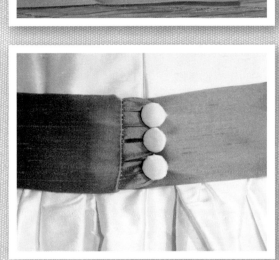

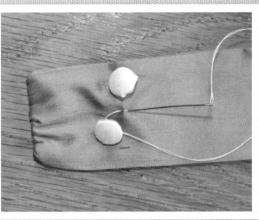

19a   19b

17 Fold up the hem on the fold of the contrast fabric and zigzag stitch it to the main fabric seam allowance.

18 Now for the sash. Cut a length of contrast fabric. It should be twice the desired width plus two seam allowances. The length should be the waist measurement, plus 2in (5cm) and two seam allowances.

Make three covered buttons and measure them to see the length of rouleau needed for your button loops. Attach the loops to one end of your sash (see pages 44–46).

19 Seam down the long side, leaving a small opening in the centre to pull the sash through to the right side. Now sew the end seams, pull the sash through and hand-sew the opening closed.

Lastly, have a fitting to see where the buttons need to go before sewing them on (**19a** and **19b**).

And see what you've made – you should be very proud of yourself! You can add a separate net underskirt as well if you like (see page 48).

Bluebell 3

This dress is quite the opposite of the last one. It looks very simple but in fact it can be quite tricky. This dress will test your cutting and sewing skills and accuracy is of prime importance. It will help if you go back to the basic sewing section and revisit sewing curves in opposite directions (see pages 19–23).

1

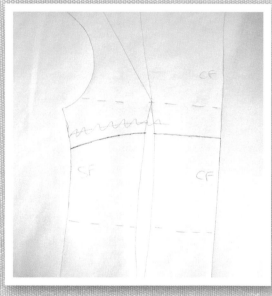

2

1 Trace round the front of the basic block as it is. There's no need to throw any darts at this stage.

2 Draw in the top line of your contrast band. Of course, you could make this straight, but I've chosen to make things slightly more challenging and have added a curve.

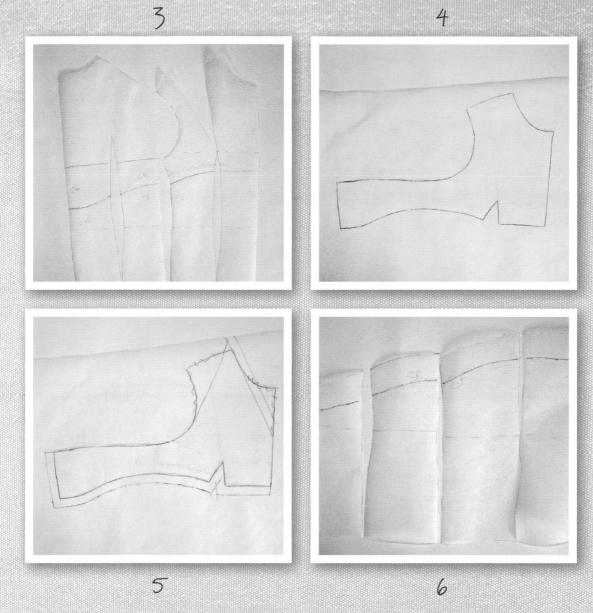

5   6

3 Do the same for the back, making sure that the lines all join up. It may help to measure down from the underarm and the top of the darts.

4 Cut out the top of the bodice along the new line. Join up the side seams and darts and close the shoulder dart at the front to open the waist dart. Retrace the shape.

5 Draw in the desired arm and neckline shape. Add seam allowance to the hem, back seam and neckline and that's your first pattern piece done.

6 Take the leftover pattern pieces and draw in the bottom line of the contrast band. This can be any shape you want it to be; I've drawn mine parallel to the top line.

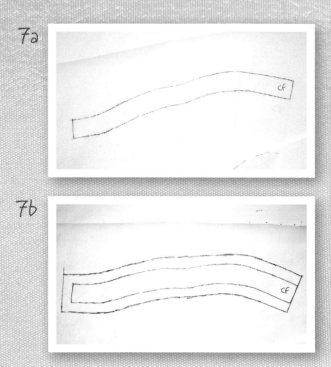

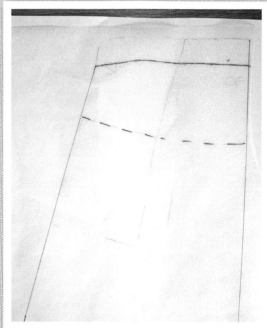

7b

7 Cut out the band pieces, join the seams and darts together to form the band shape, then trace onto fabribaste (**7a**). Add seam allowance, smoothing out any sharp points. (**7b**).

8 Now for the skirt pattern. Join the remaining centre-front block to the side-front block at the band line. Open up the dart to make an A-line shape. Trace round, extending the centre-front and side lines down to the required length plus ½in (1cm).

9 Add seam allowances to the side seam and the contrast line seam. Now do the same for the back. Remember to add your seam allowance at the centre-back seam as well. Cut out.

That's your pattern done, let's make the dress!

9

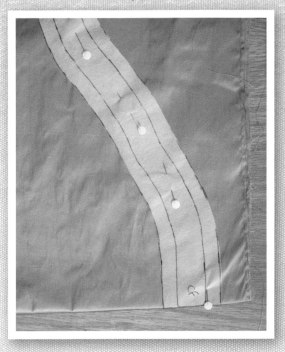

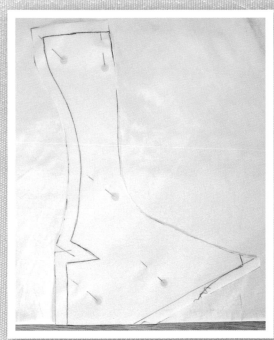

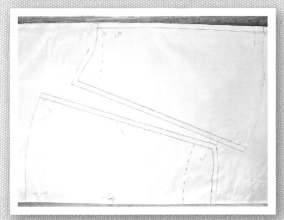

10 Cut out your contrast band, placing the centre-front line on the fold of the fabric. You will also need a band for the lining.

11 Cut out the bodice, placing the centre-front line on the fold of the main fabric. Cut another bodice for the lining.

12 Cut out your skirt, placing the centre-front line on the fold of the fabric again. You will find that if you turn the back pattern piece through 180 degrees, it will fit in the space left by the front skirt and you will save fabric. Cut another skirt in lining fabric, making it ½in (1cm) shorter at the hem.

13 Mark in and sew the bust darts on both the main fabric and the lining.

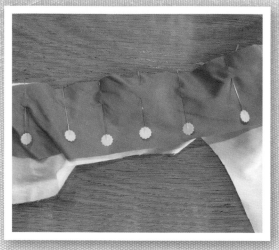

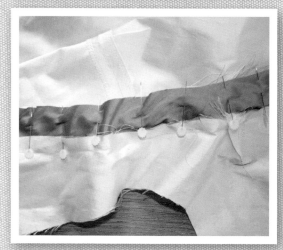

15a

15b

14 Using the curve-to-curve technique (see page 20), pin and sew the contrast band to the bottom of the bodice (**14a** and **14b**).

If your cutting and sewing skills are accurate, the back seams will join up exactly. Notch and press the seams towards the darker fabric

15 Overlock the side seams of the skirt. With right sides together, sew the side seams and press. Attach the skirt to the contrast band of the bodice using the curve-to-curve technique (see page 20) (**15a** and **15b**).

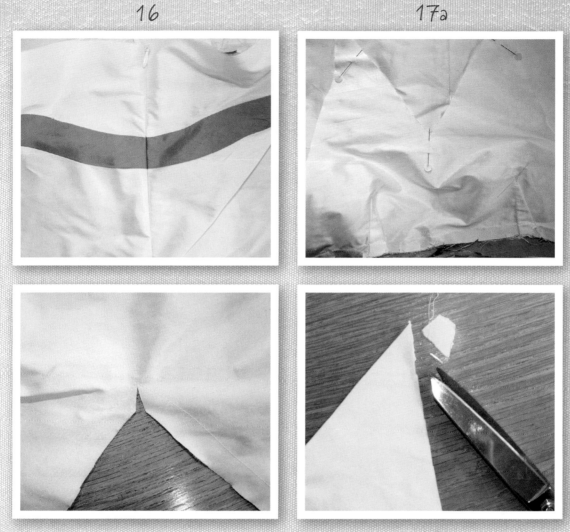

16 Insert a concealed zip (see page 40). The contrast band should meet exactly, if sewn properly. If not, take it out and do it again!

17 Make up the lining with a contrast band exactly as we did for the main dress. When you sew the back seam, leave an opening the same length as the zip.

Next, with right sides together, pin the main bodice to the lining bodice at the neckline (**17a**).

Stitch, leaving your needle down and pivoting at the centre front. Snip into the 'V' (**17b**).

18 Turn through and press. Cut off the little 'bunny ears' that stick out from the seam at the top neck.

19

20a

20b

21

19 Fold the back lining in by ⅝in (1.5cm) at the centre-back seams and, with *wrong sides together*, pin the main bodice to the lining at the top.

20 Cut a length of bias binding 1½in (4cm) wide. The binding has to be long enough to go from the centre-back seam to the shoulder edge, and carry on down to the top of the dress at the back, plus a little extra. Fold in one long edge by ½in (1cm) and press. With right sides together, pin the unfolded edge of the bias to the top seam, folding a little round to the back, at the start and end of the seam (**20a**).

Turn the binding to the inside and hand-sew in place (**20b**).

21 When you get to the free edge of the binding, fold it in half and continue sewing the binding together. Now repeat for the other side.

22

23

24

25

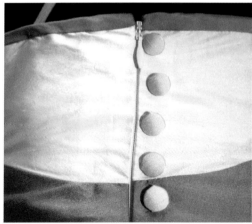

22 For the little bow (or you could use a fabric flower) cut a rectangle of fabric. It needs to be as wide as the required bow plus seam allowances by twice the length plus seam allowances.

Fold in half from top to bottom and machine-stitch both ends. Turn through, press and hand-stitch the opening closed.

Run a gathering stitch up the centre of the bow.

23 Wrap a little of your leftover bias strip round the centre of the bow and securely hand-stitch it in place on your dress.

24 Try the dress on and hand-stitch the straps in place, crossing over at the back.

25 Sew on some covered buttons, spacing them evenly.

Bias-bag the hem on the main dress (see page 38). Turn and overlock the hem on the lining and the dress is done!

Lavender

'Lavender's blue, dilly dilly,
Lavender's green,
When I am king, dilly, dilly,
You shall be queen.'

LAVENDER BLUE
English Folk Song

Lavender

Every now and then, a princess needs
a quick-to-make dressing-up outfit.
This dress is perfect for a fancy
dress party, a school play or even an
unexpected invitation to the palace!

This dress utilizes a combination of techniques that you've already done, so you should find it really easy to make. As a little test of your understanding of my techniques, try and work out how the dress is cut and made before you read the instructions. I think you'll be really surprised by how much you already know.

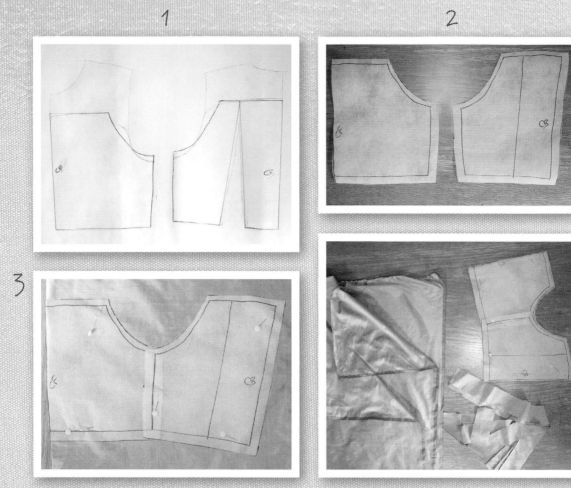

The dress

1 Start by taking your back and front blocks and trace around them, throwing the darts into the waist. Draw in the bodice shape as shown.

2 Close up the back dart (not the front one). Add seam allowance and cut out. Remember to mark the centre back and centre front on the pattern, as the pattern pieces look quite similar.

3 The point of this design is speed. Any seams that you can join up at this stage will make construction much quicker.
Lay out your front and back pieces on the main fabric and place the side seam lines together – that's two fewer seams to sew!

4 Cut out two bodices, one for the main fabric and one for the lining.

Cut out three lengths of fabric for the skirt, the length of the required skirt length plus two seam allowances by the full width of the fabric.

Cut out four strips of fabric for the shoulder straps, the width of the required strap plus two seam allowances by the length of the required strap plus 4in (10cm).

5

6

7

8

5 With right sides together, sew down both long sides of the shoulder straps. Turn through to the right side and press.

6 With right sides together, sew the skirt sections together, leaving the back seam open. You don't need to finish the seams, as they are cut with the selvedge in place.

Little Tip

To save even more time, use a nice satin or velvet ribbon for the straps.

However, to save on miles of frayed edges, overlock or overcast the top and bottom edges of the skirt and also the bottom edges of the bodice.

Gather the skirt on to the bodice, just as we did for the *Bluebell* dresses. Leave about 1in (2.5cm) ungathered at the back seams.

7 Sew the seam and press towards the bodice.

8 Now, with right sides together, pin the shoulder straps to the front bodice. If you are placing them right to the edge, as on my design, you will need to leave a seam allowance gap at the edges, as shown.

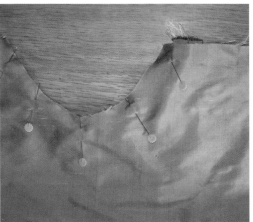

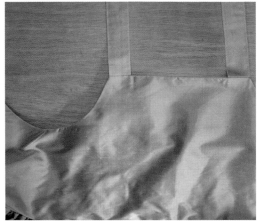

11a   11b

9 Place the bodice lining face down on to the main bodice and pin into place. Sew across the top of the bodice, being careful not to catch any of the loose straps in the seam.

10 Clip the curves and snip the corners. Turn through to the right side and press.

11 Insert a concealed zip into the back seam, as we've done before (**11a**).

Hand-stitch the lining to the zip tape (**11b**).

12 Bias-bag the hem (see page 38). Rather than hand-sew the bias in, you can press the bias to the inside and then use any fancy stitch on your machine to topstitch it in place. Stitch from the right side of the fabric.

Make a sash, as we've done before. Add a net underskirt and your princess could wear it just like that. But let's take it one step further and add a sheer over-dress.

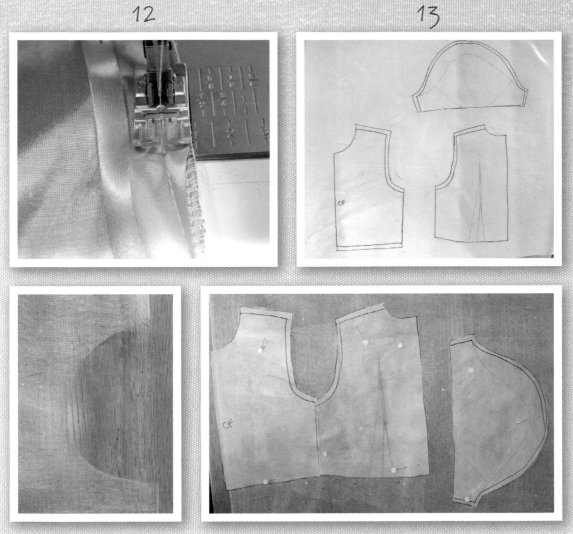

12

13

14a

14b

The over-dress

13 Trace the front and back blocks to the waist. Throw the darts into the waist. Add seam allowance to the waist, armholes and shoulder. There is no need to add a seam allowance to the back seam. Make a short sleeve pattern as for *Bluebell 1* (see page 121).

14 Cut two full-circle skirts as we did for *Bluebell 1*, but this time offset the cutout for the waist, so that the front dress length is shorter and the back skirt length longer (**14a**). Cut out the bodice and sleeves (**14b**).

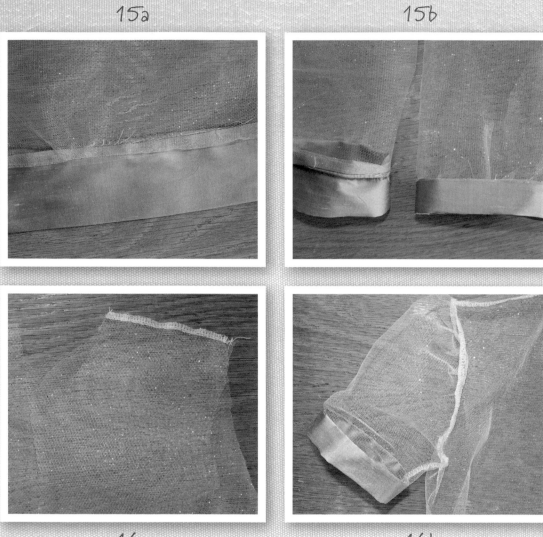

15a

15b

16a

16b

15 Make up the sleeves, just as we did for *Bluebell 1*, using some of the main dress fabric for the bands (**15a** and **15b**).

16 Sew and overlock the shoulder seams. My fabric is so sheer that I've trimmed the seams right back, as they will be seen through the net (**16a**).

Set in the sleeves (**16b**).

19a

19b

17 Use some fine ribbon to finish the edges. Zigzag or overlock the ribbon on to the right side of the bodice, down the back seams first and then round the neckline. Leave a length of ribbon free at both sides of the back neck to make the ties.

18 Sew the same ribbon around the hems of the two circle skirts.

With right sides together, pin the skirts to the waist of the bodice, making sure that the shorter length of the skirt is at the front.

19 Now the over-dress is finished (**19a**).

Use the sash from the main dress to tie at the waist and tell your little princess, 'You shall go to the ball!' (**19b**).

Lily

'The lily of the vale,
of flowers the queen,
Puts on the robe
she neither sewed nor spun'

ELEGY – WRITTEN IN SPRING
Michael Bruce

Lily

Now for something a little more taxing. This is a bodice and skirt combination that is truly spectacular. The skirt looks quite complicated but, even though it uses some couture-style techniques, if you follow the instructions carefully and give yourself plenty of time, you will be able to 'wow' everyone with your new-found designer skills.

I've used a truly beautiful silver and grey shot silk taffeta with an overlay of corded lace on the bodice. This was the most expensive dress in the book to make. For such a special dress, I urge you to use the best fabric that you can afford.

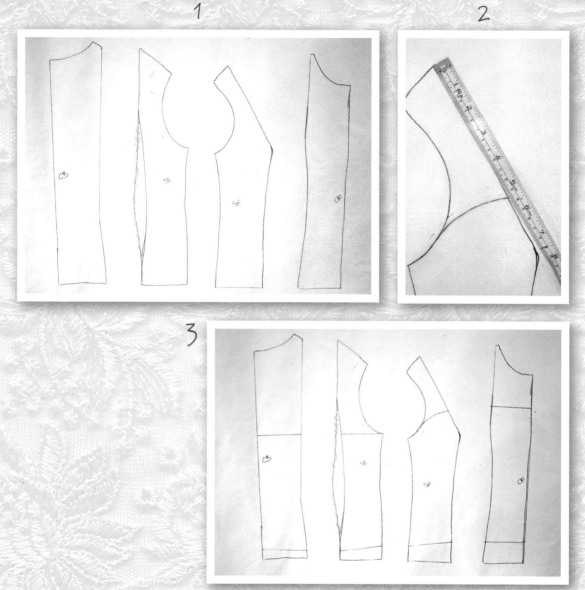

Making the pattern

1 Starting with the bodice, trace round your block right down to hip level. We are not going to throw any darts in this design.

2 Draw in your required shape for the top line of the bodice. Measure down from the shoulder to the top line, then transfer this measurement to the next piece and you will be able to line up your top line easily.

3 Do the same for the back. Then draw in the bottom line on the front and back pieces. I angled my bottom line down slightly towards the centre back.

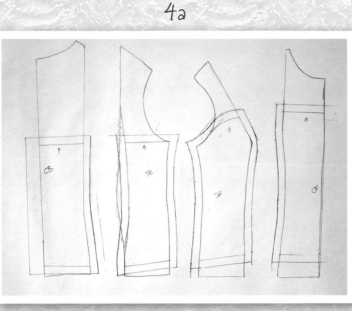

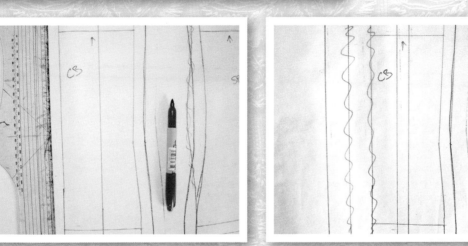

4 Add ⅝in (1.5cm) seam allowances all round (from now on we will assume this amount for all seam allowances, unless otherwise stated). Add about 2in (5cm) to the back seam for the overlap under the lacing (**4a**).

I decided to add another seam into the centre-back pieces for my lacing loops. I drew in the new seam line vertically, and added the extra seam allowances required to the centre-back seam (**4b** and **4c**).

Little Tip

If you trace a line by mistake, as I have done, cross it out with a different colour pen to save confusion later.

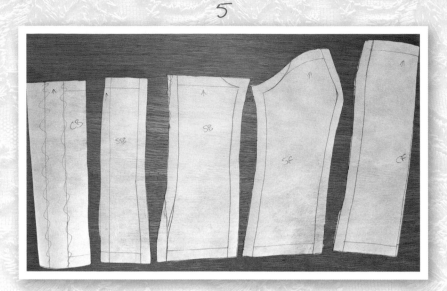

5 Cut the pieces out. You will now have a centre front, side front, centre back and two side back pattern pieces.

6 Now for the skirt pattern. Using your centre-front block piece first, trace the waistline, then throw a line out in an A-line shape from the seam.

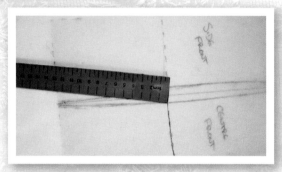

6

7 Measure down this line the length of the skirt to the floor. Draw in the hemline, making sure that the line is always the same measurement from the waist. Your line should curve out slightly (**7a**).

Next, add a seam allowance to the side and hem (**7b**).

7a

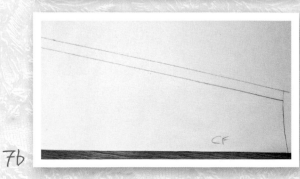

7b

8 Now do exactly the same for the side front, adding seam allowances to both seams and the hem (**8a** and **8b**).

9 Do the same for the back pieces. Mark the pattern pieces so you know which is which. Cut out the skirt pieces in the lining fabric, exactly as they are.

9

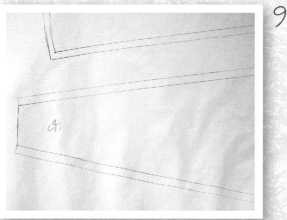

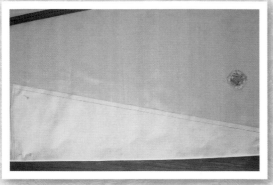

10a

10b

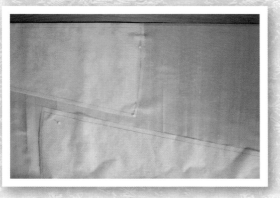

10c

11

Making the skirt

10 We are going to extend the hemline by about half the skirt length again. Pin the centre-front pattern to the fold of your main fabric (**10a**).

Measure down the side seam to the new length. This is not a critical measurement; the longer the top skirt, the more pull-ups it will have. However, be sure to use the same measurement for all of the skirt pieces (**10b**).

Flip the next pattern piece over and you will find that it should fit into the waste fabric of the first piece (**10c**).

11 Cut out all the pattern pieces this way. This is a very 'fabric hungry' skirt, so play around with the pattern until you have as little waste as possible.

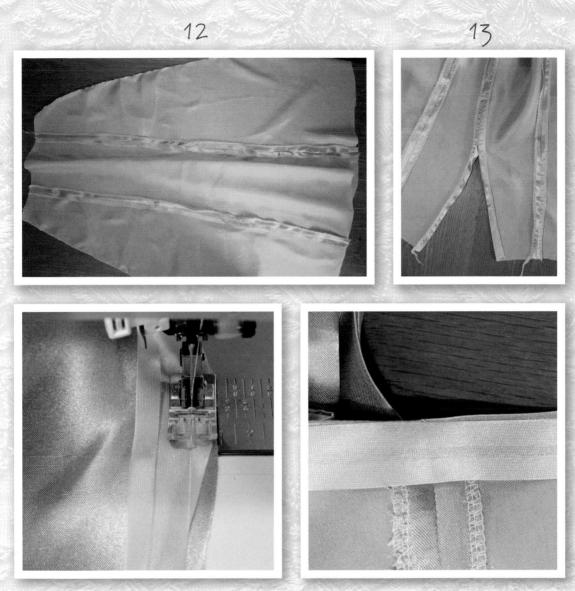

12 Overlock or overcast around all the main skirt and lining pieces. With right sides together, sew the side fronts to the centre-front linings and press the seams open.

13 Sew the side backs to the centre backs. Sew the centre-back seam, leaving an opening at the waist that is the length of your chosen zip.

14 Sew the side seams and press. Then bias-bag the hem; you can machine-stitch the bias up if you like, as it won't be seen (**14a** and **14b**).

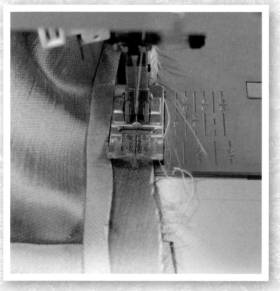

17a

17b

15 On the main skirt, set in a concealed zip in the back seam.

16 Make up the rest of the skirt exactly as for the lining. Bias-bag and hand-stitch the hem. You now have two skirts: one in lining fabric and one, which is much longer, in main fabric.

Pin the lining inside the main skirt at the waist as it will be worn, i.e. wrong sides together.

17 Next, cut some bias binding and bind the waist edge, folding the bias round at the zip, just as we've done before (**17a**).

Hand-stitch the binding to the inside (**17b**).

18 Now for the exciting part! Put the skirt on your princess and begin to drape the skirt at the seam lines by pulling up and pinning it, as shown. Be careful not to catch the lining.

19 Carry on pinning the pull-ups and make them randomly spaced. Be sure that when you have finished, the hemline is how you want it to be. I've let mine fall slightly longer at the back.

20 Reach up inside the skirt at the seams and grab the seam allowances where the first pin is. Lay them together and sew back and forth a few times to hold the pull-up in place. Remove the pin.

Continue this way until all the pull-ups are secure. Fit the skirt again and adjust if necessary.

20

21

22a

22b

23

Making the bodice

21 Cut out all your pattern pieces in the main fabric. You will need to cut the centre-back sections twice.

22 Cut off the scalloped edge of the lace, at both ends of the fabric, being sure to leave some seam allowance for sewing in later (**22a**).

Fold the remaining lace and cut out all but the centre-back pieces (**22b**).

Do the same for the lining fabric.

23 We are now going to treat the main fabric and the overlay lace as one piece. Pin the lace pieces to the right side of the corresponding main fabric pieces, being very careful not to stretch the lace.

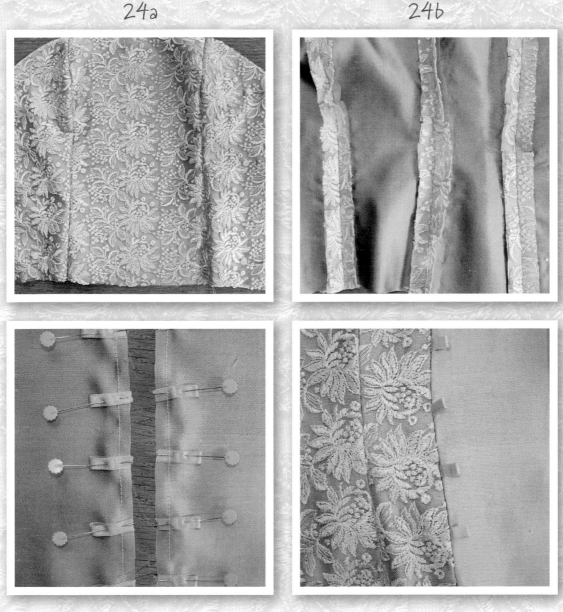

24a

24b

25a

25b

24 Now sew the side fronts to the centre front (**24a**).

Add all the side-back pieces the same way.

Snip and press the seams open, as if they were one piece of fabric (**24b**).

25 On the inside seams of the centre-back pieces pin some rouleau loops or strong satin ribbon. The loops should be evenly spaced down the seam, as shown (see page 44). Sew a ½in (1cm) seam to secure the loops (**25a**).

Sew these pieces to the main bodice (**25b**).

28 29a

26 Make up the bodice lining, adding the main fabric centre-back panels. Add a label at this stage if you like.

27 Fold in one edge of the lining by ⅝in (1.5cm) and press. Do the same for the corresponding main bodice edge when you place right sides together.

28 Take the lace scallop edge that you cut off earlier. Fold one edge in by ⅝in (1.5cm) and, with right sides together, pin the lace to the top of the bodice. Start ⅝in (1.5cm)

in from the unfolded seam of the bodice but finish on the fold the other end, folding the lace in by ⅝in (1.5cm).

29 Take two lengths of ribbon for the lacing at the back. The lacing also forms the shoulder straps, so cut the ribbons long enough to go over the shoulders and criss-cross through the loops. I cut mine at about 3yd (3m) and then trimmed them down to size later. Pin the ribbon to the front bodice where you want the strap to start (**29a**).

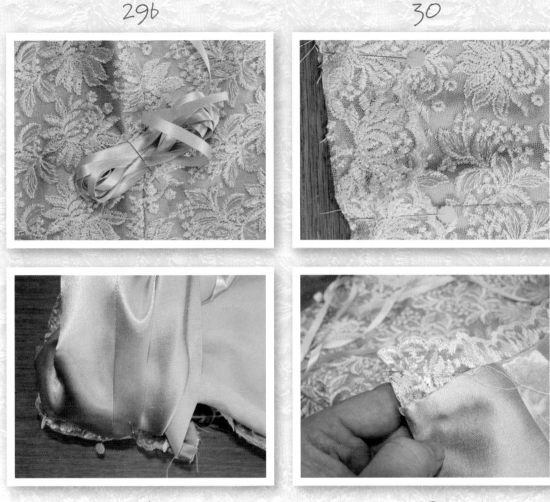

29b

30

31

32

Loop the ribbon up and pin to the bodice to keep it out of the way while you sew (**29b**).

30 Pin some more lace edging to the bottom of the bodice in exactly the same way that you did for the top.

31 With right sides together, pin and sew the lining to the main fabric. Sew across the bottom, up the unfolded side and across the top.

Snip into the curves and turn through.

32 Where the lace was folded in, fold it again to make a mitre and hand-stitch the opening closed.

Press well. Fit the dress and cut the lacing to length. Then thread some more ribbon through the loops at the waist and tie at the front in a bow.

Now stand back and admire your beautiful handiwork!

Glossary

Bagged in When all rough and wrong side seams and hems are sewn inside a lining or facing, making the inside of a garment as neat as the outside.

Bias The diagonal grain of a fabric. Also known as the cross grain.

Blade point The highest point of the shoulder blade.

Bodice The top part of a dress that fits the torso.

Body block A perfect fabric rendition of half of the body, usually made out of calico. We use this for drafting patterns for the actual garment.

Boning A rigid or semi-rigid piece of polyester, acrylic or metal, which is either sewn directly on to a seam or placed inside a casing. Used to create stiffness or support on any part of a garment, most often on strapless dresses or in corsetry.

Bust point The highest part of the bust, usually in the centre at the nipple.

Calico A stiff, undyed cotton used for making body blocks and toiles.

Couture A term that literally means seam. In modern times the term is used to describe top-end fashion and dressmaking, where most of the work is done by hand. Couture garments are often one-off pieces and as such are very expensive.

Cross grain *See* **Bias**.

Dart A method of suppressing fabric when a full seam is not required.

Designer's square Set square with cut-out curves, used in pattern cutting and drafting.

Drafting The process of drawing a pattern on pattern paper or directly on to fabric.

Dress stand Often referred to as a tailor's dummy, it is a model of a body that we can use to fit our garments.

Ease The amount of extra fabric that we incorporate into a garment to make the desired fit and allow room for movement.

Fabri-Baste A non-woven fabric-type material used for tracing patterns. It is much stronger than paper and can be reused again and again.

Facing A piece of fabric that sits on the inside of a garment, usually down the front edges or around the neck and armholes.

Fitting The process of checking the fit and hang of a garment, making any adjustments necessary.

Hem The finish on the bottom edge of a garment.

Interfacing A non-woven fabric used to stiffen or add support to various parts of a garment.

Invisible zip A zip that is concealed inside a seam, rendering it 'invisible'.

Iron shield A plastic or acrylic cover that fits on the bottom of the iron, which is used to protect delicate fabrics from damage.

Lining The fabric used on the inside of the garment.

Millinery wire Thin wire that is wound very tightly with thread, usually cotton; it is used for stiffening hat brims but can also be used to make fairy wings!

Modelling The process of draping calico on a dress stand or directly on to the body to make a pattern.

Neckline The shape of the part of the garment that fits round the neck.

Notching A method of marking the fabric within the seam allowance by snipping into it with the points of the scissors.

Offset The amount that we move a point from the centre line.

Overcast A seam finish that closely resembles an overlocked edge; the fabric is not cut, as the edge is sewn.

Overlock A neat seam finish; the raw edges are cut off whilst being sewn. Also known as serge.

Pattern A dress template used when cutting out the fabric. Usually made of paper or calico.

Right side The right side of the fabric, which will be on show on the outside of the garment.

Rouleau A thin tube of fabric used for loops or straps on fine dresses and lingerie.

Run off A term for letting the machine sew off the edge of the fabric, usually in darts.

Seam Where two or more pieces of fabric are joined.

Seam allowance The amount of fabric used for sewing a seam. Usually ½in (1cm) or ⅝in (1.5cm) from the edge of the fabric.

Selvedge The thickest, strongest edge of a length of fabric.

Serge See **Overlock**.

Sleeve block A pattern for making a garment sleeve.

Sleeve head The curved top edge of the sleeve that fits into the shoulder edge of the bodice.

Snip A little cut made with the points of the scissors.

Straight grain The straight grain of fabric runs in the same direction from top to bottom or side to side.

Suppression The amount of fabric taken out of part of a garment to facilitate fit.

Tailoring shears Large scissors used only for cutting fabric.

Toile A rough rendition of the finished garment, usually made in calico.

Toile stage The stage at which the garment is cut and made in calico for fitting purposes.

Wrong side The side of the fabric that will not be seen, on the inside of a garment.

Zigzag A stitch that swings from side to side.

Acknowledgements

GMC Publications would like to thank the following

Chris Gloag for fashion photography.

Bethany, Emily, Lili and Mary for modelling, and their friends and family for all their help.

Jeni Dodson for hair and make-up.

Emma Foster and Rebecca Mothersole for help with the photoshoot and for still life photography.

Photo credit
Page 118, bluebells: istockphoto.com/ AtWaG

4x5 FILM

Author's acknowledgements

I knew that writing books would be stressful, but I never imagined that I would have a heart attack whilst writing this one! A massive thanks to all of the doctors, nurses and staff who looked after me in hospital. Thank you to all of my friends for the love and support when I got out. Big thanks once again to Sarah, my 'right hand'; all the responsibility of looking after the shop once again fell on you and you took it, as usual, in your stride.

As always, Gerrie Purcell for being fabulous and Jonathan Bailey for soothing my nerves, and to both of them and 'J.P.' for giving me the chance to share my work with you. Massive respect to Gilda Pacitti and the art department for their beautiful design of all three of my books. Thank you to Virginia, Emma and all of the girls at GMC for putting up with my diva strops. To my editor, Rachel Netherwood, and my new Senior Project Editor, Dominique Page (fairy sister),

I'm sure that I must have been a pain, but we got through it. Big thanks to Georgina Lord and everyone in marketing; without you, no one would know about me or my books.

Very special thanks to Norman Smith who taught me lots about the technical side of taking photographs. No one told me when I started out on my adventures into writing books that I would have to learn what on earth 'white balance' and 'focal length' was, but you made it seem easier.

As ever, to Clive, my civil partner and best friend; I promise I'll stop writing soon, (or at least slow down a bit). I love you. I'm sorry my heart frightened you.

And last, but by no means least, huge thanks to you, my readers. Without you buying my books, I wouldn't be able to write more of them (keep buying and I'll keep writing... but don't tell Clive!).

As always, love and happy sewing – Simon.

Suppliers

Fabrics

WWW.ABAKHAN-ONLINESHOP.CO.UK/
ACATALOG/DRESS.HTML
Always lots of clearance lines; keep
visiting the site for the best deals.

WWW.CANDH.CO.UK
A good, all-round selection of
fabrics at very keen prices.

WWW.CHEAPFABRICS.CO.UK
Good-quality fabrics at very
reasonable prices. Look out for silks
and calico here.

WWW.DERBYCLOTHHOUSE.CO.UK
For beautiful couture fabrics.

WWW.KLEINS.CO.UK
Lots of hard-to-find haberdashery
including millinery wire.

WWW.MACCULLOCH-WALLIS.CO.UK
For beautiful, top-end fabrics. Expect to
pay top-end prices but they're well worth it.
Also stock millinery supplies and tools.

Pattern-making supplies

WWW.MORPLAN.CO.UK
Excellent for design equipment
and consumables.

WWW.SHOBENFASHIONMEDIA.COM/
Pattern books and designer's set squares.

Machines

WWW.BROTHERMACHINES.COM

WWW.HOME-SEWING.COM/ENG/INDEX.PHP
For Toyota sewing and overlock machines.

WWW.HUSQVARNAVIKING.COM

WWW.JANOME.CO.UK

WWW.PFAFF.COM

Index

To request a full catalogue of GMC titles, please contact:

GMC Publications Ltd, Castle Place,
166 High Street, Lewes, East Sussex,
BN7 1XU, United Kingdom
Tel: +44 (0)1273 488005
Fax: +44 (0)1273 402866

www.gmcbooks.com